Super Minds

SECOND EDITION 2

Student's Book

Herbert Puchta · Peter Lewis-Jones · Günter Gerngross

CAMBRIDGE
UNIVERSITY PRESS

Map of the book

Back to school (pages 4–9)

Vocabulary	Language focus	Story
The classroom	• There's a (cap). There are some (pictures). • Imperatives	The burglars **Value** Helping people

▶ Song: The Super Friends

1 My day (pages 10–21) — How do we know the time?

Vocabulary	Language focus	Story	Skills	Think and learn
Daily routines	• Telling the time • Present simple, 3rd person	*What a day!* **Value** Offering to help **Phonics** The letter sounds *ee* and *ea*	• Reading and writing • Listening and speaking	Maths: Time

▶ Song: What's the time? ▶ Creativity: Create that! ▶ Revision: Think back

2 The zoo (pages 22–33) — Where do animals live?

Vocabulary	Language focus	Story	Skills	Think and learn
Animals	• likes / doesn't like • Questions and answers with Does … like?	*The zoo keeper* **Value** Helping people **Phonics** The letter sounds *ie* and *y*	• Reading, listening and writing • Listening and speaking	Environmental studies: Habitats

▶ Song: The zoo ▶ Creativity: Do that! ▶ Revision: Group check

3 Where we live (pages 34–45) — How can we find places?

Vocabulary	Language focus	Story	Skills	Think and learn
Places in a town	• Has … got … ? • Prepositions	*The tree on the track* **Value** Perseverance **Phonics** The letter sounds *tr*, *gr* and *dr*	• Reading, speaking and writing • Listening	Geography: Places in town

▶ Song: A friend from the town ▶ Creativity: Create that! ▶ Revision: Think back

4 The market (pages 46–57) — How can we buy food?

Vocabulary	Language focus	Story	Skills	Think and learn
Food	• Would you like … ? • Are there / Is there any … ?	*Bad apples* **Value** Cheating doesn't pay **Phonics** The letter sounds *w* and *wh*	• Reading, speaking and writing • Listening	Maths: Weights

▶ Song: Super fruit and vegetables ▶ Creativity: Do that! ▶ Revision: Group check

5 My bedroom (pages 58–69)
❓ What does furniture look like?

Vocabulary	Language focus	Story	Skills	Think and learn
Furniture	• this, that, these, those • Whose … is this? / Whose … are these?	Story: Tidy up! Value: Tidiness Phonics: The letter sound oo	• Reading • Listening, speaking and writing	Science: Materials

▶ Song: Wood, wood, wood ▶ Creativity: Create that! ▶ Revision: Think back

6 People (pages 70–81)
❓ How are faces different?

Vocabulary	Language focus	Story	Skills	Think and learn
The face	• Am / Is / Are + adjective • The months; our, their	Story: Thunder's birthday Value: Being a good loser Phonics: The letter sounds a_e, ai and ay	• Reading and writing • Listening and speaking	Art: Portraits

▶ Song: My face ▶ Creativity: Do that! ▶ Revision: Group check

7 Off we go! (pages 82–93)
❓ Where can transport go?

Vocabulary	Language focus	Story	Skills	Think and learn
Transport	• I'd like to … • Questions and answers with verb + ing	Story: The bus trip Value: Being generous Phonics: The letter sounds u_e, ew, ue and oo	• Listening and speaking • Listening, reading and writing	Geography: Transport

▶ Song: Far or near ▶ Creativity: Create that! ▶ Revision: Think back

8 Sports club (pages 94–105)
❓ What do we need to play sports?

Vocabulary	Language focus	Story	Skills	Think and learn
Sport	• ing forms • like + ing	Story: The football club Value: Including people Phonics: The letter sounds o, oa, and o_e	• Listening, speaking and writing • Reading	Physical education: Sports equipment

▶ Song: Let's play! ▶ Creativity: Do that! ▶ Revision: Group check

9 Holiday plans (pages 106–117)
❓ What makes a good holiday?

Vocabulary	Language focus	Story	Skills	Think and learn
Holidays	• Can for requests • Revision	Story: Dream holidays Value: Teamwork Phonics: The letter sounds z and s	• Reading • Listening and speaking	Environmental studies: Helping the environment

▶ Song: Holidays are the best ▶ Creativity: Create that! ▶ Revision: Think back

• **Language focus:** (pages 118–128)   • **Stickers:** (page 129)   Practice of creative thinking, critical thinking and cognitive skills

Map of the book 3

Back to school

1  **Listen and look. Then listen and say the words.**

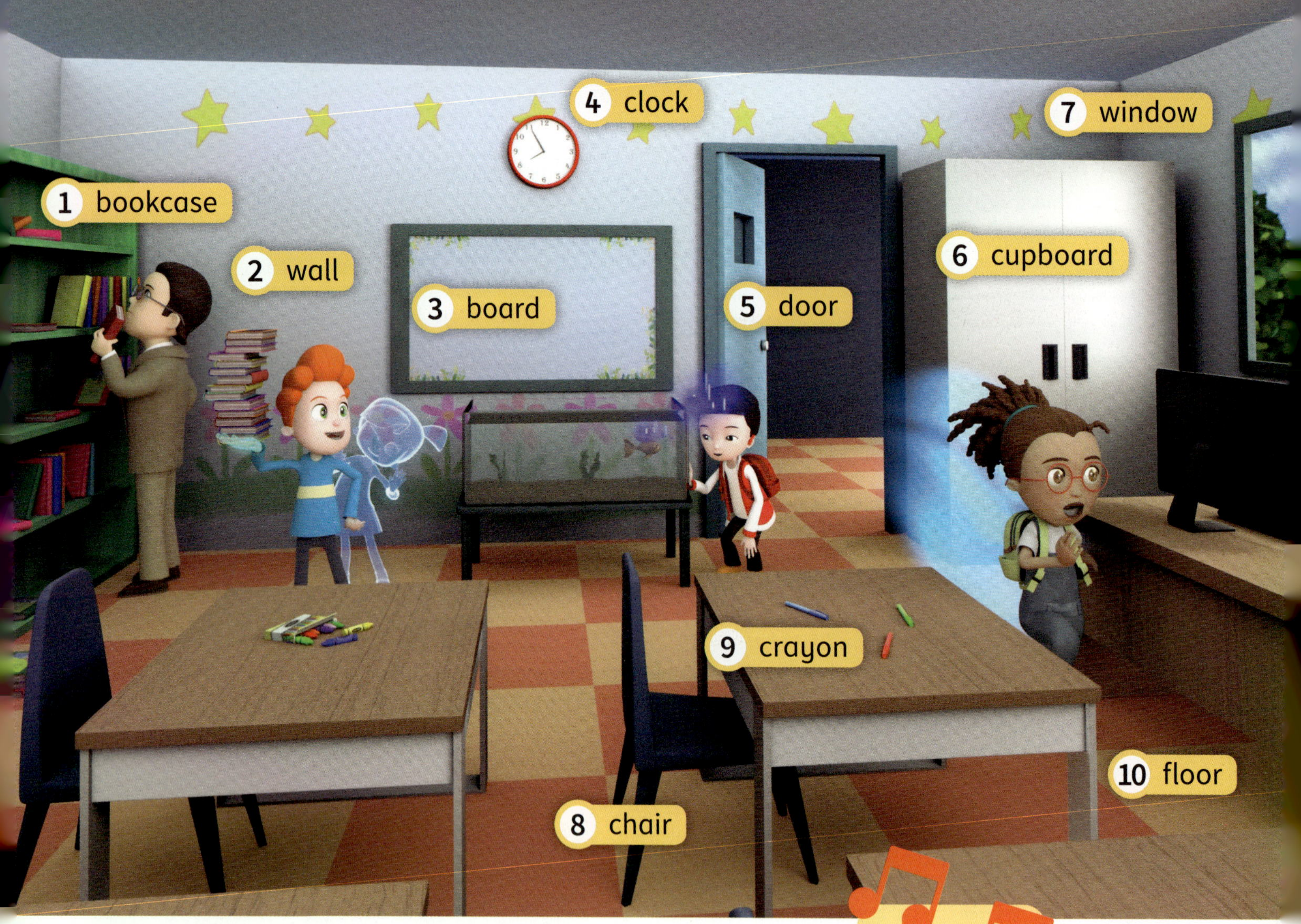

1 bookcase
2 wall
3 board
4 clock
5 door
6 cupboard
7 window
8 chair
9 crayon
10 floor

2  **Listen and chant.**

Walk to the window.
Walk to the door.

Touch the cupboard.
Jump on the floor.

Walk to the bookcase.
Walk to the wall.

Look at a crayon.
And that's all!

4 The classroom

1 Look, read and tick ✅.

1 ☐ There are some crayons.
2 ☐ There's a clock.
3 ☐ There are some rulers.
4 ☐ There's a rubber.
5 ☐ There are some books.
6 ☐ There's a pencil case.

2 ▶ 🎧 003 Watch, listen and say.

> **Language focus**
>
> **There's a** cap on the floor.
> **There are some** pictures on the wall.
> **There's a** bed by the door.
> But that's not all, that's not all.
>
> **There's a** bookcase with some books.
> Come closer. Take a look.
> **There's a** big clock. **There's a** chair.
> Can you guess who's there?

3 🛡 Close your eyes. Listen to your teacher and answer.

There's a board in the classroom.

There's / There are

1    **Listen and sing. Then number the pictures.**

10, 20, 30, 40, 50!
The Super Friends are in the city.
60, 70, 80, 90!
Thunder, Flash, Whisper, Misty.

Count from one to ninety-nine.
The Super Friends are feeling fine.
Now from ninety down to ten.
The Super Friends are back again.

Misty's number's 22.
You don't see her, but she sees you.
Whisper's number's 66.
He can talk to ducks and chicks.

10, 20, 30, 40, 50!

Count from one to ninety-nine ...

Thunder's number's 33.
He can lift a big, big tree.
And Flash's number's 88.
She's so fast, she's really great.

2 **Work with a friend. Draw numbers in the air and guess.**

Is it 55?   No, it isn't.   Is it 88?   Yes, it is!

6 Singing for pleasure; numbers 10 to 100

1 🎧 006 Listen and number the pictures. Then read and draw lines.

a Sit down.
b Open your book.
c Don't sit down.
d Don't stand up.
e Don't open your book.
f Stand up.

2 ▶ 🎧 007 Watch, listen and say.

Language focus

Open the book. **Open** the book, please.
Stand up. **Stand up**, please.
Don't sit down! **Don't** sit down, please!
Yes!

3 Play the listening game.

Stand up.

Imperatives 7

The burglars

1 🎧 008 ▶ **What do the burglars take from the school?**

1

Thunder, Flash and Whisper: Bye!
Misty: Now let's go home.

2

Bird: Whisper, there's a problem at your school.
Whisper: Let's go to the school. Quick!
Misty: Now?

3

Whisper: Can you check this out, Flash?
Flash: No problem.

4

Flash: There are two burglars taking our computer.
Thunder: What can we do?
Misty: I've got an idea. Wait here!

5

Misty: Oooooh!
Tall burglar: What's that?

6

Misty: Aaargghh!
Short burglar: There are some monsters in here.
Tall burglar: Let's go!

8 Value: helping people

Thunder: The burglars!
Tall burglar: Don't drop the computer!
Short burglar: OK.

Tall burglar: Close the door!
Short burglar: OK!

Thunder: We've got them!

Officer 1: Well done.
Officer 2: Great work.
Super Friends: Yes!

2 Read and correct the mistakes.

There's a problem at the Super Friends' school. There are three burglars! The burglars are taking a computer. They've got two cars. The burglars drop the computer. Then the children stop the burglars.

1 My day

1 🎧 009

Listen and look. Then listen and say the words.

1 get up
2 get dressed
3 have breakfast
4 brush your teeth
5 go to school
6 have lunch
7 play in the park
8 have dinner
9 go to bed

BIG QUESTION How do we know the time?

2 🎧 010 Listen and chant.

Get up early,
Yawn, yawn, yawn.
Have your breakfast,
Crunch, crunch, crunch,
Brush your teeth,
Brush, brush, brush.

Go to school,
Run, run, run.
Have some lunch,
Munch, munch, munch.
Go out and play,
Hip, hip hooray!

10 Daily routines

1 🎧 011 Listen and draw lines.

2 ▶ 🎧 012 Watch, listen and say.

Language focus

When do you have breakfast?
At eight **o'clock**.

What's the time?
It's eight **o'clock**.

3 Ask and answer. Then draw the times on the clocks.

When do you … ?

At … o'clock.

get up   have breakfast

go to school   go to bed

Telling the time 11

1 🎧 013 ▶ Listen and sing. Then draw the times on the clocks.

What's the time in Brazil?
What's the time in Brazil?

It's nine o'clock in Brazil.
Nine o'clock's so cool.
It's nine o'clock in Brazil.
It's time to go to school.

What's the time in Turkey? ...

It's three o'clock in Turkey.
My friends are all with me.
It's three o'clock in Turkey.
It's time to watch TV.

What's the time in China? ...

It's eight o'clock in China.
The moon is very bright.
It's eight o'clock in China.
It's time to say 'goodnight'.
Stop!

2 🛡 What things do you do at the same time every day?

*Every day, I get up at seven o'clock.
I have breakfast at eight o'clock.*

1 Read and number the pictures.

Amelia gets up at six o'clock. She walks to school at nine o'clock. After school, she meets her friend Ellie. At five o'clock, Amelie plays with Ellie in the park. Then they listen to music in Amelia's house. Amelia has dinner at eight o'clock.

2    Watch, listen and say.

Language focus

Penny **walks home** at seven o'clock.
She **has her dinner** at eight.
Then she **watches some TV**
And **goes to bed**. It's late!

She's very tired at nine o'clock.
She **goes to sleep** at ten.
She **sleeps and sleeps** and then
It's time to get up again!

3 Look and say what the children do.

Present simple, 3rd person 13

What a day!

1  What does Thunder have for dinner?

1 Thunder: Oh no!

2 Thunder: Not again.

3 Misty: Careful, Thunder.
Thunder: Oops!

4 Thunder: What's the problem, Mum?
Mum: Can you see my keys? They're under the car.

5 Mum: Careful, Thunder!
Thunder: Sorry, Mum.

6 Thunder: Mmm! I love chicken. It's not such a bad day after all.

Thunder: Bedtime. Hurray!

Thunder: No!

2 What does Thunder do at these times?

1 seven o'clock
2 four o'clock
3 six o'clock
4 three o'clock
5 eight o'clock

> Thunder … at seven o'clock.

Phonics

3 Find who says …

> Can you s**ee** my k**ey**s?

4 🎧 017 Listen and say.

At thr**ee** o'clock, I **ea**t my ch**ee**se and p**ea**s and then I cl**ea**n my t**ee**th.

Phonics focus: the letter sounds *ee* and *ea*

Skills

1 Read and circle.

Sam is a firefighter. His house is in Cambridge, but he works in London. At seven o'clock, he leaves his home and walks to the train. Then he takes the train to London. He arrives at eight o'clock. Sam works in a team with 11 friends. At five o'clock, Sam leaves work. At six o'clock, his train leaves London. Then he arrives in Cambridge at seven o'clock. He gets home at eight o'clock. He wants to go to sleep! What a long day for Sam!

1 Sam leaves his house.

2 He arrives in London.

3 He leaves work.

4 His train leaves London.

5 The train arrives in Cambridge.

6 Sam gets home.

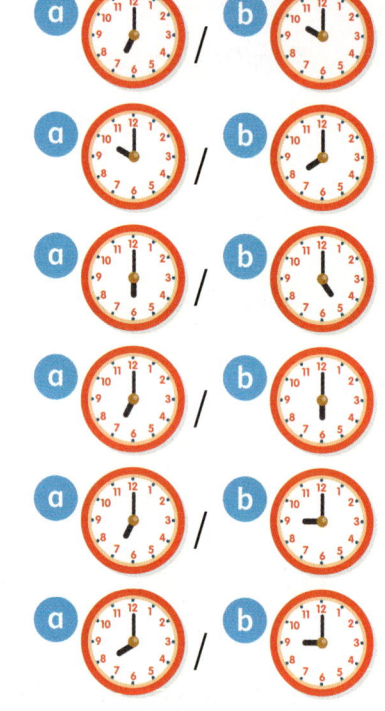

2 Draw and write about your favourite day of the week.

My favourite day is Monday. I get up at seven o'clock. I have breakfast at eight o'clock. Then I go to school. I like school. My favourite class is on Monday morning. It's English! I get home at four o'clock. I do my English homework.

16 Reading and writing

1 🎧 018 Listen and draw the times.

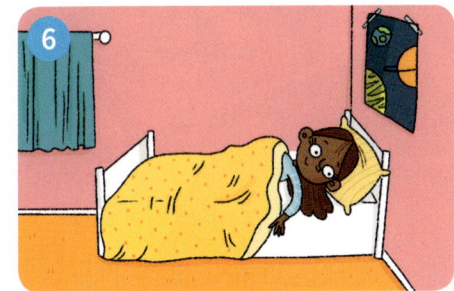

2 Talk about your day.

"I get up at … I have breakfast at …"

Listening and speaking

Think and learn

▶ **What kinds of clocks are there?**

1 🎧 019 **Listen and point.**

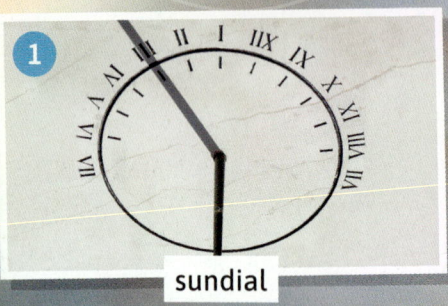
1 sundial

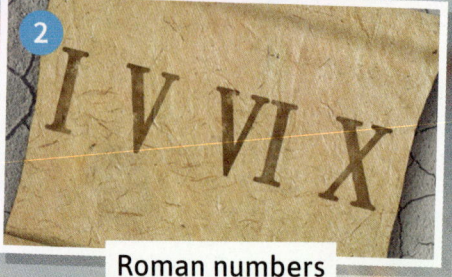
2 Roman numbers

3 5 o'clock

4 6 o'clock

5 sun

6 shadow

2 Read and look.

Here are the Roman numbers from 1 to 12.

There are different systems to show the time. A sundial is an old clock. It's got a metal arm and a round face with Roman numbers. The sun makes a shadow with the metal arm. The shadow falls on the Roman numbers and shows the time.

I = 1   V = 5   IX = 9
II = 2   VI = 6   X = 10
III = 3 VII = 7 XI = 11
IV = 4   VIII = 8 XII = 12

🎧 020 **Now listen and write the Roman numbers.**

a ___V___   c _____   e _____   g _____
b _____   d _____   f _____   h _____

3 **Add and write the correct Roman numbers.**

1 I + IV = ___V___   3 III + I = _____   5 IX − II = _____
2 V + V = _____   4 X + II = _____   6 IV − III = _____

18 Maths

4 What time is it on the sundials? Ask and answer.

> What time is it on sundial 1?
>
> It's 3 o'clock.

5 Write the times of the sundials.

1. It's __3 o'clock__.
2. It's _____.
3. It's _____.
4. It's _____.
5. It's _____.
6. It's _____.

6 ⭐ **Project** Draw and write about a sundial with Roman numbers.

My Sundial

Six o'clock is my favourite time.
The Roman number for six is VI.
I have dinner at six o'clock.

Create that!

1 🎧 021 Listen and imagine. Then draw your picture.

2 Work with a friend. Compare your pictures.

> In my picture, I'm in … It's … o'clock.
> In your picture, you're …

Think back 1

1 Read and circle.

1 I … at seven o'clock in the morning.
 a get dressed   b get up   c have breakfast

2 I … at eight o'clock in the evening.
 a go to school   b brush my teeth   c have dinner

3 When … you brush your teeth?
 a do   b doing   c does

4 … the time?
 a When's   b What's   c Is

5 He … to bed at ten o'clock.
 a going   b go   c goes

6 She … in the park at five o'clock.
 a plays   b playing   c play

7 In the story, … helps get Mum's keys from under the car.
 a Misty   b Whisper   c Thunder

8 What time is it on the sundial?
 a It's 6 o'clock.   b It's 9 o'clock.   c It's 11 o'clock.

2 The zoo

1 🎧 022 **Listen and look. Then listen and say the words.**

1. polar bear
2. bear
3. zebra
4. crocodile
5. hippo
6. tiger
7. parrot
8. monkey
9. snake

BIG QUESTION Where do animals live?

2 🎧 023 **Listen and chant.**

Come on, let's go to the zoo,
The animals are there for you.

Hippo, monkey, parrot, too.
Polar bear in the zoo.

Zebra, tiger, snake and bear.
A crocodile is also there!

Come on, let's go to the zoo,
The animals are there for you.

1 Look, read and write the names.

1 Monica the monkey likes bananas.
2 Mary the monkey doesn't like cheese.
3 Tony the tiger likes chicken.
4 Tim the tiger doesn't like carrots.
5 Ben the bear likes apples.
6 Bill the bear doesn't like peas.

2 024 Watch, listen and say.

Language focus

Penny **likes** fish.
She **doesn't like** peas.
Don't give Penny
Any peas, please!

Penny **likes** fish.
She **doesn't like** cheese.
Don't give Penny
Any cheese, please!

3 Draw an animal. Tell a friend about it.

This is Simon the snake. He lives in the grass. He eats frogs and spiders. He doesn't like apples and bananas.

1 🎧 025 ▶ Listen and sing. Then tick ✓ the animals in the song.

Snakes like grass
And tigers do too.
They like life
Here in the zoo.
Snakes like grass ...

In the zoo, in the zoo
Here in the zoo
Yes, they like life
Here in the zoo.

Bears like trees
And parrots do too.
They like life
Here in the zoo.
Bears like trees ...

In the zoo, in the zoo ...

Crocodiles like water
And hippos do too.
They like life
Here in the zoo.
Crocodiles like water ...

In the zoo, in the zoo ...

2 Look, think and draw. Which animals like ...

water	grass	trees

1 🎧 027 **Listen and circle.**

1 Does the baby tiger sleep a lot? a Yes, it does. b No, it doesn't.
2 Does it eat meat? a Yes, it does. b No, it doesn't.
3 Does it play? a Yes, it does. b No, it doesn't.
4 Does it like swimming? a Yes, it does. b No, it doesn't.

2 ▶ 🎧 028 **Watch, listen and say.**

Language focus

Does Penny **like** crocodiles?   **Does** Penny **like** hippos?
No, she **doesn't**.   No, she **doesn't**.
Does Penny **like** snakes?   **Does** Penny **like** polar bears?
No, she **doesn't**.   Yes, she **does**!

3 **Look at the table. Ask and answer.**

Does Ryan like snakes?   Yes, he does.

Questions and answers with *Does … like?*

The zoo keeper

1   Which animals can you see in picture 8?

1 **Thunder:** Look at the monkey.

2 **Zoo keeper:** Help!
Flash: The zoo keeper doesn't know what to do.
Thunder: Let's help him.

3 **Flash:** Got you!
Zoo Keeper: Wow!

4 **Zoo Keeper:** How does he do that?

5 **Whisper:** Come here, Snake.
Snake: Yes, Whisper.

6 **Zoo Keeper:** No, my keys! Don't throw them.
Misty: I can help.

Value: helping people

Thunder: Great, Misty.

Misty: Here you are.
Zoo Keeper: Thank you all so much!

2 Match the Super Friends with the animals.

Phonics

3 Find who says … M**y** keys!

4 🎧 030 Listen and say.

Don't tr**y** and sm**ile** at m**y** crocod**ile**, M**i**k**e**!

Phonic focus: the letter sounds *i_e* and *y*

Skills

1 Read and tick ✓ the boxes.

Green Bay Safari Park

Come and see our animals! Which is your favourite? Is it the tiger? The zebra? The hippo? What about crocodiles? Or snakes? We've got lots of different animals.

Take your car through our beautiful park and have a great time. Get near to the animals. Imagine you're in Africa. Our park rangers can answer all your questions about our animals.

You can come to our restaurant for lunch, too. We've got sandwiches, pizza and chicken and lots of other great food and drink.

Open: 10:00 to 6:00

1 The park opens at 6:00.   ☐ yes ☐ no
2 There's a hippo at the park.   ☐ yes ☐ no
3 You can talk to the park rangers.   ☐ yes ☐ no
4 There isn't food at the park.   ☐ yes ☐ no

2 🎧 031 Listen and answer.

1 What's the crocodile's name?
2 Where's he from?
3 How old is he?
4 What's his favourite food?

3 Write about an animal. Say and guess with a friend.

My favourite animal is very big. It likes meat, but it doesn't like water. What is it?

1 🎧 032 ✏️ **Listen and stick.**

2 **Look and say.**   The cheese is …

Think and learn

▶ **What habitats are there?**

1  **Listen and point.**

polar habitat

grassland

rainforest

ocean

2 Look, read and say what habitats the animals live in.

Animals live in different habitats. A habitat is a home for plants and animals. There are lots of different habitats. Some are very cold like the polar habitats and some are hot like the grassland and rainforest habitats. Some are water like the ocean habitat. They are all habitats where animals live.

Zebras live in grassland.

zebra	crocodile	monkey	fish	polar bear	lizard
grassland	grassland	grassland	polar habitats	polar habitat	grassland
	rainforest	rainforest	rainforest		rainforest
			ocean		

3 Draw a penguin and a parrot in their habitats.

penguin

parrot

30 Environmental Studies

4 **What habitats do you think these animals live in? Tell a friend.**

> I think elephants live in …

	elephant	tuna fish	frog	butterfly	snake
polar habitat					
grassland					
rainforest					
ocean					

🎧 034 Now listen and tick ✓.

5 **Project** Draw a habitat with three different animals. Write about your picture.

This is a rainforest habitat. It is hot here. There are snakes, parrots and monkeys here.

Environmental Studies 31

Do that!

1 🎧 035 Listen and act out with your teacher. Then listen again and number the pictures.

2 Read the sentences from the story and draw lines.

a Oh no! The monkey's got it!

b Hey, where's the banana?

c You're hungry. Peel a banana.

d Watch the monkey in the tree.

e You are at the zoo. Look around.

f Eat your banana.

3 🛡 Listen to a friend and act it out.

You are at the park. Look around.
There's a duck in the pond.
You're hungry. Eat some bread.
Oh no! The duck's got it!

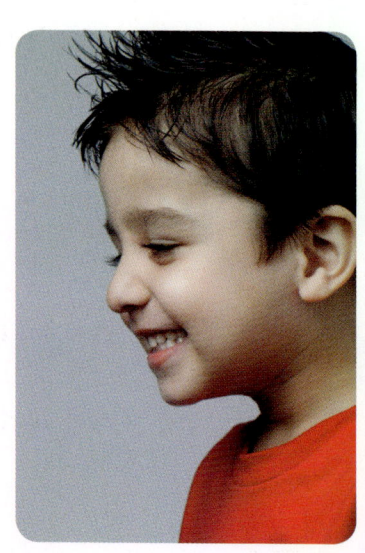

Creativity

Group Check Units 1 and 2

1 How many words can you remember? Draw pictures.

Daily routines

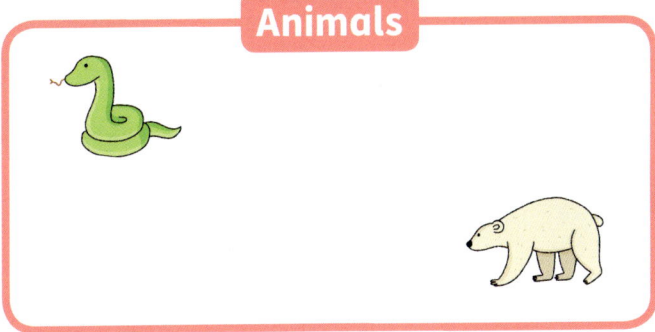

Animals

2 Write and say the words.

3 🎧 036 Listen and number.

No? Do you like snakes? ☐

Me too! ☐

Look! Jane likes snakes. [1]

Yes. But she doesn't like hippos or tigers. ☐

Yes, I think they're nice. ☐

4 Write a new dialogue. Act it out.

💬 Look! _____ likes _____ .

💬 Yes. But _____ doesn't like _____ or _____ .

💬 No? Do you like _____ ?

💬 Yes, I think they're nice.

💬 _____

Revision 33

3 Where we live

1. 🛡 🎧 037 **Listen and look. Then listen and say the words.**

1. train station
2. hospital
3. cinema
4. playground
5. café
6. shop
7. street
8. bus stop
9. park
10. school
11. swimming pool

BIG QUESTION How can we find places?

2. 🎧 038 **Listen and chant.**

There's a park in our town,
A playground and a cinema, too.
There's a café on the street.
Let's go there, me and you!

There's a shop in our town,
A bus stop and a train station, too.
A hospital, a swimming pool.
Let's go there, me and you!

34 Places in town

1 Look at the picture. Read and circle.

1 Has Top Town got a cinema? Yes, it has. / No, it hasn't.

2 Has Top Town got a café? Yes, it has. / No, it hasn't.

2   039 Watch, listen and say.

> **Language focus**
>
> **Has** your town **got** a cinema?
> No, it **hasn't**!
>
> **Has** your town **got** a swimming pool?
> Yes, it **has**!

3 Imagine a town and write five things it has got. Then ask and answer.

Has your town got a hospital?

No, it hasn't. It's got …

Has … got … ? 35

1 **Listen and sing. Then draw lines.**

It's good to have a friend from the town.
Listen carefully and write it down.
Please write it down.

Has your town got a playground? ○
Yes, it has, Sue.
Please tell me how to get there
I can go with you.

It's good to have a friend …

Has your town got a bookshop? ○
Yes, it has, Jack.
Please tell me how to get there.
I can draw it on my map.

It's good to have a friend …

Has your town got a café? ○
No, it hasn't, Jack and Sue.
But let's go to my house.
There's cake and fruit for you.

It's good to have a friend …

2 **Write a new verse for the song.**

Has your town got _____?

Please tell me how to get there.
I can go there with you.

Singing for pleasure

1 🎧 042 Write the words. Then listen and check.

1 The café is between the _____ and the cinema.
2 The car is in front of the _____.
3 The hospital is next to the _____.
4 The tree is behind the _____.

2 ▶ 🎧 043 Watch, listen and say.

> **Language focus**
>
> The fish is **next to** the rock. The fish is **behind** the rock.
> The fish is **in front of** the rock. The fish is **between** the tree and the rock.

3 🧽 Decide where to stick these places on your map. Then tell a friend.

Where's your hospital?   It's next to the café.

Prepositions

The tree on the track

1 🎧 044 ▶ **Which pictures show a tree on the train track?**

1

Thunder: Look. The train is leaving the station.
Misty: But there's a tree on the track!

2

Whisper: Run, Flash! Run and stop the train!
Flash: OK.

3

Flash: Stop! Stop the train!
Driver: Wow. She's fast!

4

Flash: It's no good. Hmm. Let's try something else.

5

Driver: She's next to my train again. What does she want?

6

Driver: S–T–O–P.

38 Value: perseverance

7

Flash: Stop!

8

Driver: Thanks, kids!
Flash: No problem.

2 Point to pictures in the story and make sentences.

The Super Friends are	on	the hill.
The driver is	next to	the train.
The tree is	in front of	the track.
Flash is	in	the station.
The train is		the town.

Phonics

3 Find who says …   But there's a **tr**ee on the **tr**ack!

4 🎧 045 Listen and say.

In **Tr**icia's play**gr**ound, there's a **gr**een **dr**um and a **gr**ey **tr**ain.

Phonics focus: the letter sounds *tr*, *gr* and *dr*

Skills

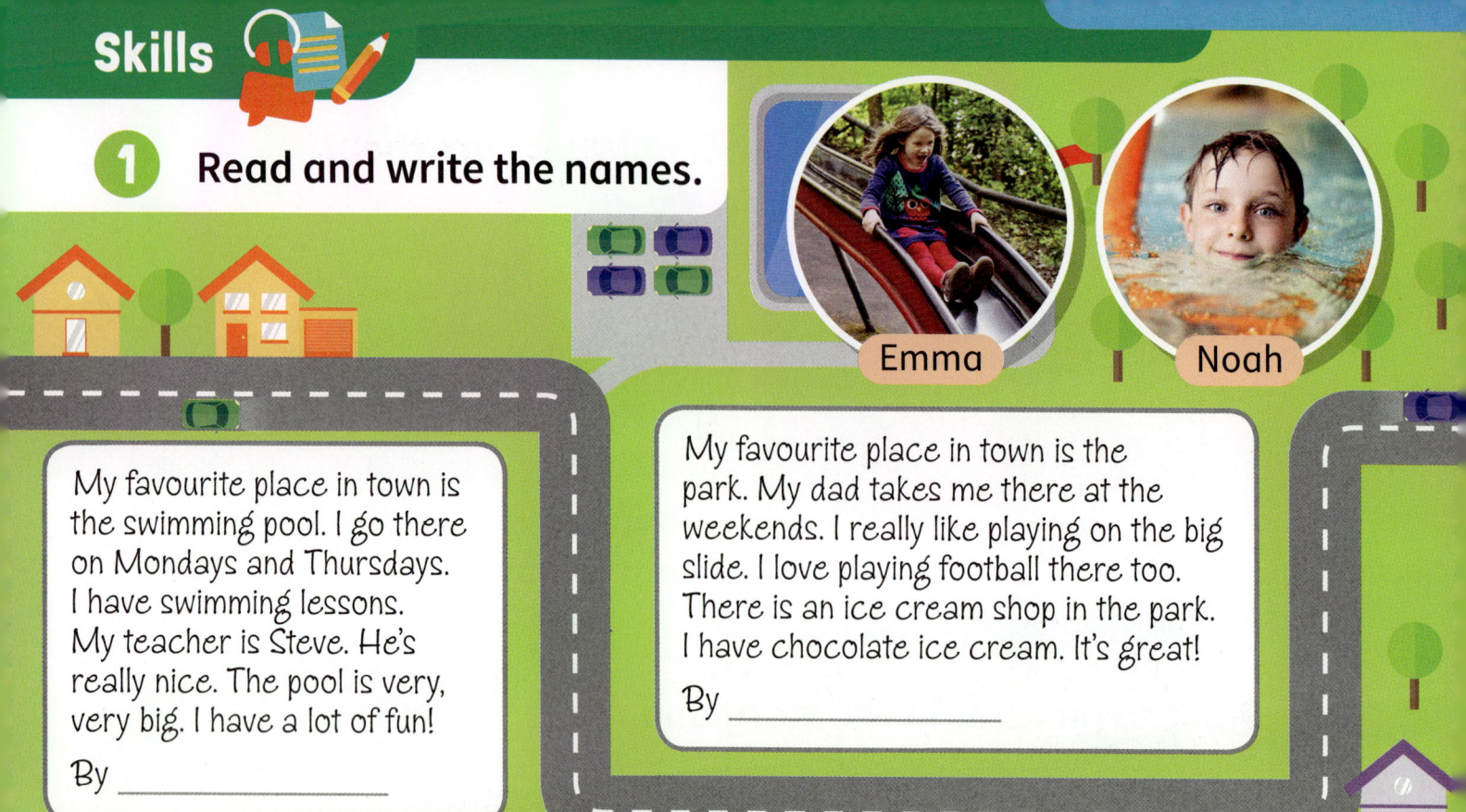

1 Read and write the names.

Emma　　Noah

My favourite place in town is the swimming pool. I go there on Mondays and Thursdays. I have swimming lessons. My teacher is Steve. He's really nice. The pool is very, very big. I have a lot of fun!
By _____

My favourite place in town is the park. My dad takes me there at the weekends. I really like playing on the big slide. I love playing football there too. There is an ice cream shop in the park. I have chocolate ice cream. It's great!
By _____

2 Read again and answer the questions.

1 Which days does Noah go to the swimming pool?
2 What's his swimming teacher's name?
3 Who does Emma go to the park with?
4 What does Emma eat in the park?

> Noah goes to the …

3 Draw and write about your favourite place.

My favourite place is Madrid. It's a beautiful city in Spain. I go there to see my cousin. He lives there with his family. I like the Prado. It's a famous museum.

4 Now tell a friend.

> My favourite place is …

40　Reading, speaking and writing

3

1 🎧 046 Listen and tick ✓ the box. Where are they?

1.
   a. bus stop
   b. zoo
   c. bookshop

2.
   a. playground
   b. café
   c. farm

3.
   a. hospital
   b. cinema
   c. train station

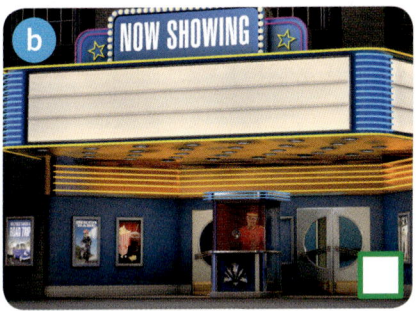

4.
   a. swimming pool
   b. school
   c. bus stop

Listening 41

Think and learn

Places in town

▶ What's in towns?

1 🎧 047 Listen and point.

1. monument
2. sports centre
3. car park
4. museum
5. market

2 Has your town got these places? Where are they?

> My town has got a museum. It's next to the cinema.

3 Look and read. Where is the café? What is it next to?

We can find places on some maps with letters and numbers. Say the number first, then the letter. On this map, the school in square 3D. The café is in square 3A.

Geography

4 Look at Activity 3 again. Ask and answer.

1 What's in square 2D?
2 What's in square 3C?
3 Where's the market?
4 Where's the train station?

What's in square 2D?

There's a …

5 Read and think. Draw lines.

In towns, there are places to eat, places to do sport, places to buy food and go shopping. There are lots of places in towns to have fun. There are also places to learn like schools and museums and places, like hospitals, for people to get help.

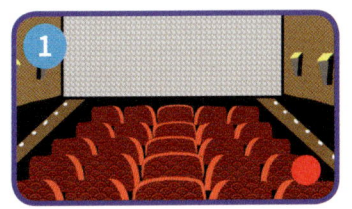

- a watch films and learn
- b play and have fun
- c learn interesting things
- d go shopping

6 Project Design a town.

- Choose six places
- Draw a map and a grid
- Name your town
- Talk about your town

The name of my town is Kids Town. It's got a sports centre in square 2A. You can do sport there.

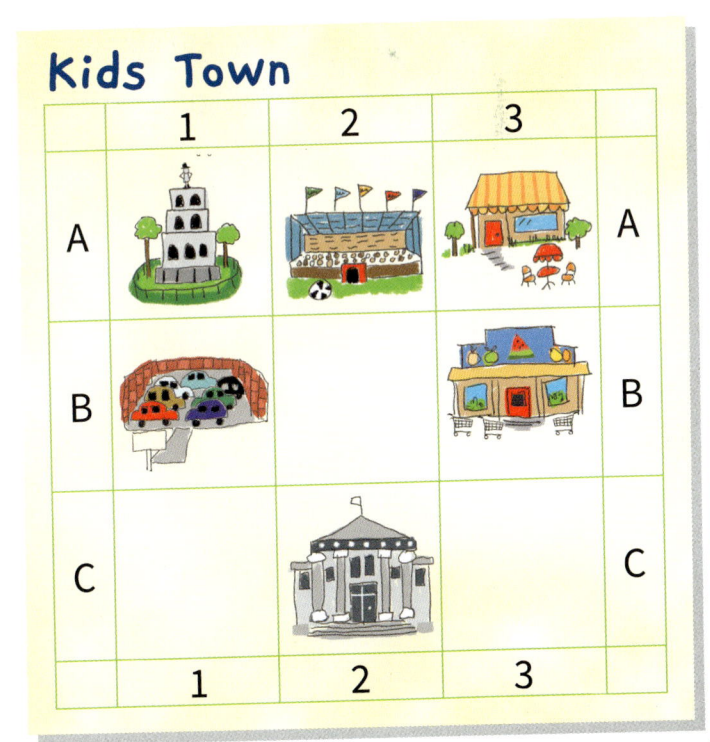

Kids Town

Geography

Create that!

1 🎧 048 🛡 **Listen and imagine. Then draw your picture.**

2 **Work with a friend. Compare your pictures.**

> In my picture, I'm with Penny at …
> We're next to …
> In your picture, you're …

Creativity

Think back 3

1 Read and circle.

1. The ... is next to the park.
   a playground   b swimming pool   c hospital

2. The ... is behind the bus stop.
   a cinema   b shop   c school

3. Has the street got a train station?
   a Yes, it has.   b No, it hasn't.

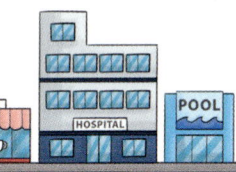

4. Has the street got a school?
   a Yes, it has.   b No, it hasn't.

5. The café is ... the school.
   a behind   b next to   c in front of

6. The bus stop is ... the shop and the cinema.
   a next to   b behind   c between

7. In the story, there's a ... on the track.
   a car   b tiger   c tree

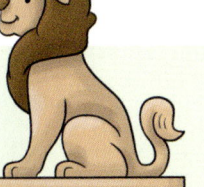

8. This is a ...
   a monument.   b car park.   c museum.

Revision 45

4 The market

1 🎧 049 Listen and look. Then listen and say the words.

1. tomatoes
2. beans
3. greens
4. potatoes
5. kiwis
6. lemons
7. bread
8. mangoes
9. grapes
10. eggs
11. watermelons

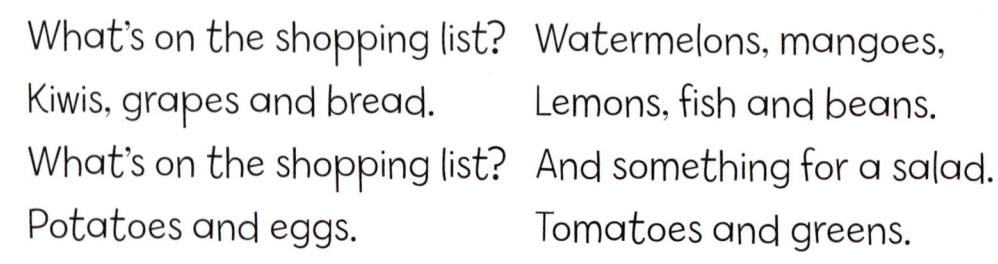

BIG QUESTION How can we buy food?

2 🎧 050 Listen and chant.

What's on the shopping list?
Kiwis, grapes and bread.
What's on the shopping list?
Potatoes and eggs.

Watermelons, mangoes,
Lemons, fish and beans.
And something for a salad.
Tomatoes and greens.

Food

1 Read and number the pictures.

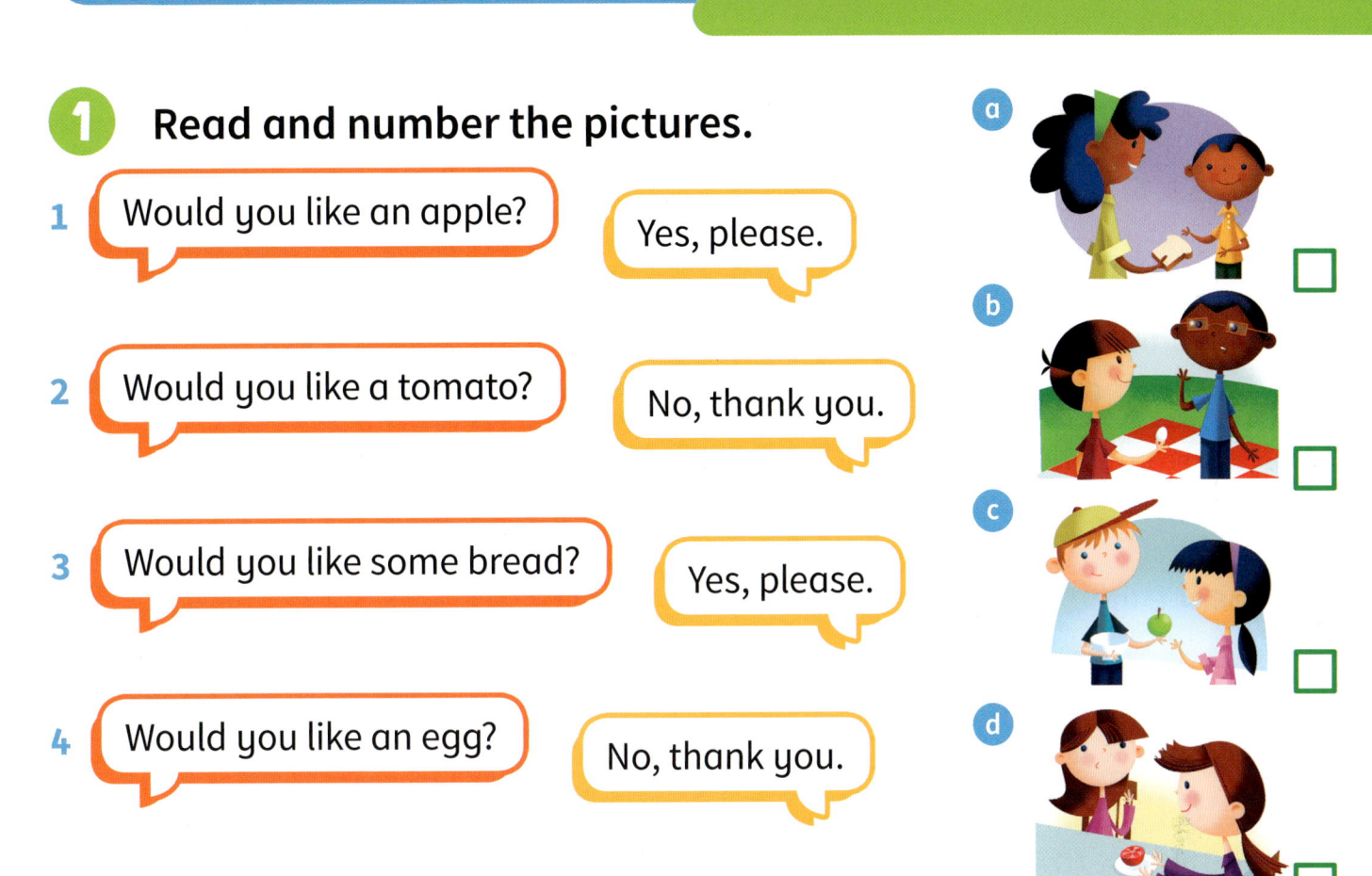

1. Would you like an apple? — Yes, please.
2. Would you like a tomato? — No, thank you.
3. Would you like some bread? — Yes, please.
4. Would you like an egg? — No, thank you.

a
b
c
d

2 051 Watch, listen and say.

Language focus

Would you **like** a pizza, Penny?
Yes, please.
Would you **like** some bread?
Yes, please.

Would you **like** some ice cream?
No, thank you. I think I need my bed.

3 Tick ✓ four things you would like to eat. Then ask and answer.

Would you like … ? 47

1 🎧 052 ▶ **Listen and sing. Then listen and tick ✓ the food you hear.**

Would you like an apple?
Would you like a pear?
There's lots of fruit and vegetables
Lots for us to share.

Super fruits and vegetables
Pick them from the tree
Lemons, pears and mangos, too.
Pick one for you
And one for me.

Would you like an apple …

Super fruits and vegetables
Grow them in the ground
Carrots, peas, potatoes, too
There's good food all around.

Would you like an apple …

2 🛡 **Ask and answer.**

> Which fruit and vegetables grow on trees?

> Which fruit and vegetables grow in the ground?

> Which fruit and vegetables grow on plants?

48 Singing for pleasure

1 Look, read and tick ✓.

1 Are there any eggs in the fridge?
  ☐ Yes, there are.   ☐ No, there aren't any.

2 Are there any apples in the fridge?
  ☐ Yes, there are.   ☐ No, there aren't any.

3 Is there any cheese in the fridge?
  ☐ Yes, there is.   ☐ No, there isn't any.

4 Is there any water in the fridge?
  ☐ Yes, there is.   ☐ No, there isn't any.

2 ▶ 🎧 054 Watch, listen and say.

Language focus

Is there any cheese in the house?
No, there **isn't any**.
Yes, there **is**.

Are there any grapes in the house?
No, there **aren't any**.
Yes, there **are**.

3 Stick your food. Then ask and answer.

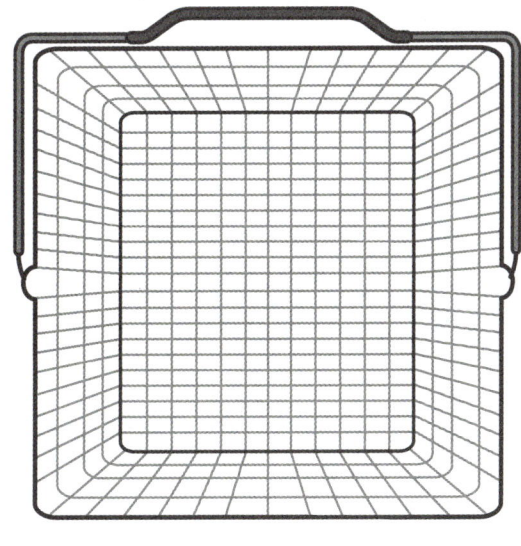

Are there / Is there any … ? 49

Bad apples

1 🎧 055 ▶ **Which fruit can you see in the story?**

1
Flash: Here are two apples for everyone.

2
Thunder: Look! I've got a bad apple.
Misty: Me too.
Whisper: So have I.

3
Whisper: What can we do?
Misty: I've got an idea. Come to the market with me.

4
Man: Apples. Nice, sweet apples!

5
Misty: The man has got a box with good apples and a box with bad apples.
Flash and Thunder: We know what we can do.

6
Flash: Eight apples, please.
Man: Here you are.

50 Value: cheating doesn't pay

7

Flash: Look everybody!
Whisper: Four bad apples!

8

Thunder: A box of good apples and a box of bad apples.
Woman: Well done, children!

2 Look at the picture and choose the correct sentence.

1 Look everybody!
2 Two for everyone.
3 Well done!
4 Come to the market with me.

Phonics

3 Find who says …

What can **w**e do?

4 🎧 056 Listen and say.

Where's the **w**atermelon, **W**ally?

Phonics focus: the letter sounds *w* and *wh*

Skills

1 What's needed for the chocolate cookies? Read and tick ✓.

☐ butter   ☐ sugar   ☐ chocolate chips   ☐ flour   ☐ an apple   ☐ an egg   ☐ peas

1 Melt the butter.

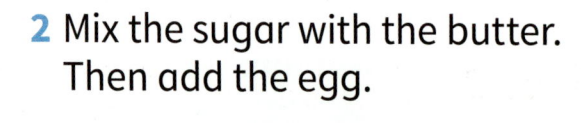

2 Mix the sugar with the butter. Then add the egg.

3 Mix in the flour and the chocolate chips.

4 Make small balls and put them on a tray.

5 Bake in the oven for ten minutes.

2 Read and act it out.

Boy: Let's make fruit salad for the party.
Girl: OK.
Boy: Hello. I'd like some apples, please.
Man: How many?
Girl: Four. And we'd like some bananas.
Man: How many?
Boy: Two. Have you got any grapes?
Man: Sorry. We haven't got any.
Girl: Have you got any mangoes? 
Man: Sorry. No mangoes.
Girl: Thank you. Let's go to another shop.

3 Write your own play and act it out.

1 🎧 **057** **Listen and tick ✓ the boxes.**

1 What does all the family like?

a ☐   b ☐   c ☐

2 What vegetables does Mum cook?

a ☐   b ☐   c ☐

3 What does Dad not like?

a ☐   b ☐   c ☐

4 What does Sandra like?

a ☐   b ☐   c ☐

Listening 53

Think and learn

WEIGHTS

▶ How can we get fruit and vegetables?

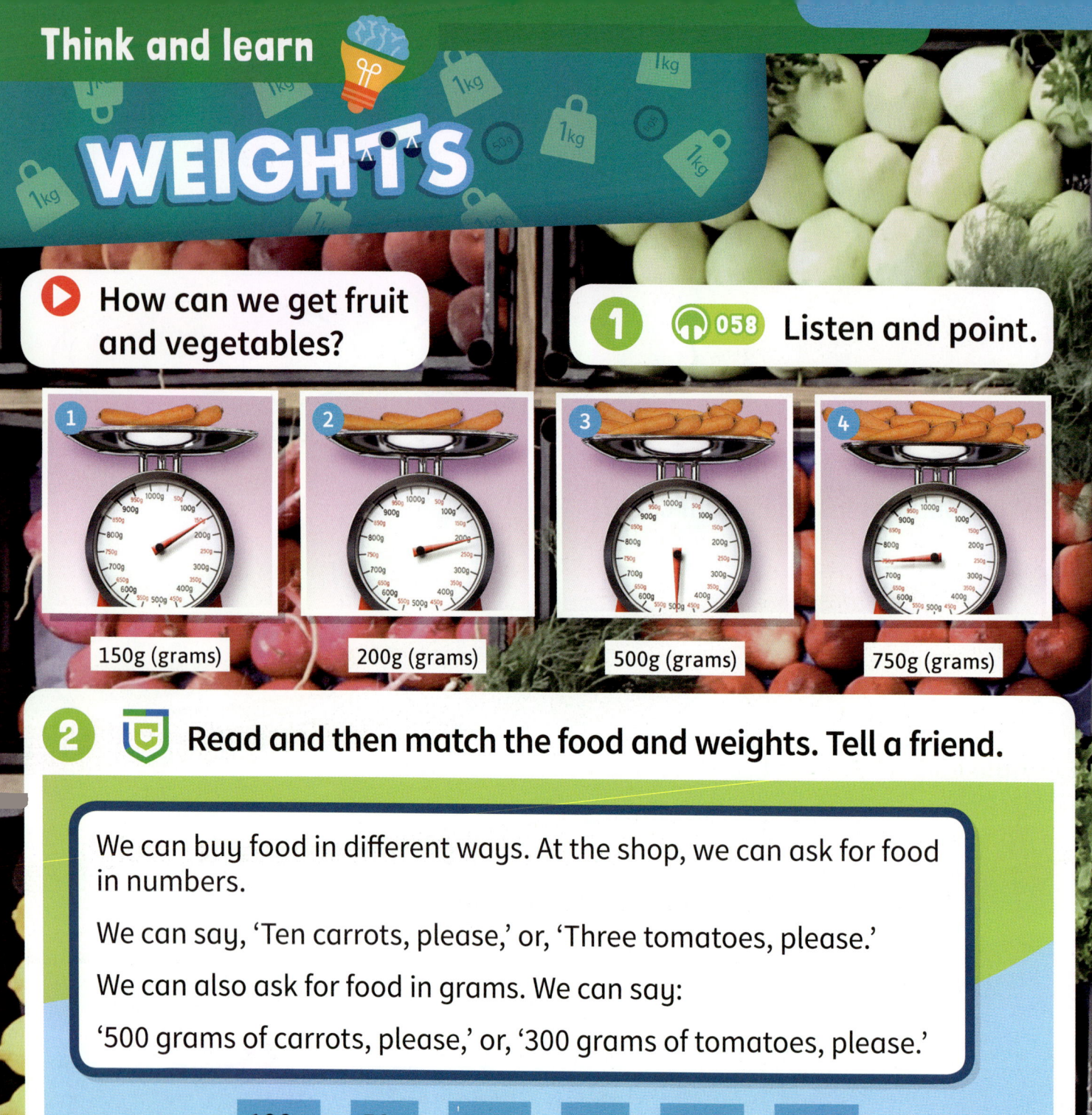

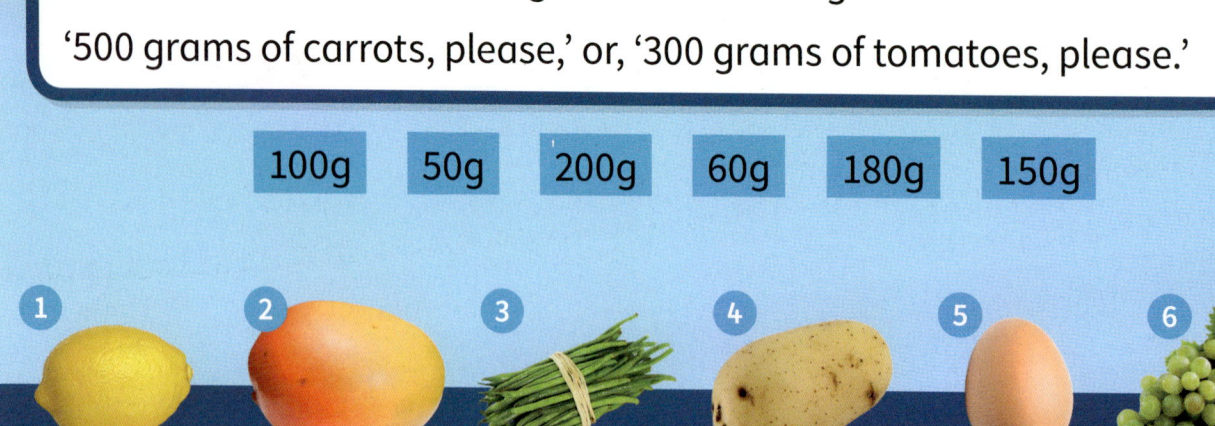

1 🎧 058 Listen and point.

1. 150g (grams)
2. 200g (grams)
3. 500g (grams)
4. 750g (grams)

2 Read and then match the food and weights. Tell a friend.

We can buy food in different ways. At the shop, we can ask for food in numbers.

We can say, 'Ten carrots, please,' or, 'Three tomatoes, please.'

We can also ask for food in grams. We can say:

'500 grams of carrots, please,' or, '300 grams of tomatoes, please.'

100g 50g 200g 60g 180g 150g

1. lemon
2. mango
3. chives
4. potato
5. egg
6. grapes

I think the lemon weighs 50 grams.

3 How many grams of fruit and vegetables are there?
Do the food sums.

1. 700g + 250g = _____ g of vegetables

2. 200g + 450g = _____ g of fruit

3. 200g + 150g = _____ g of vegetables

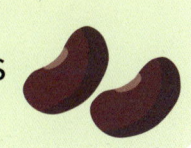

4. 500g + 300g = _____ g of fruit and vegetables

4 ⭐ Project Find out how much fruit and vegetables weigh. Then draw and write two food sums.

The watermelon weighs 500g.
The bananas weigh 300g.
500g and 300g make 800g.
I've got 800g of fruit!

The apple weighs 150g and the orange weighs 100g.
I've got 250g of fruit.

Do that!

1 🎧 059 **Listen and act out with your teacher. Then listen again and number the pictures.**

2 Read the sentences from the story and draw lines.

a A fish! Oh no! Take it out.

b Get some grapes. Put them in.

c Peel a banana. Put it in.

d Get a fish. Throw it in.

e Get a bowl for a fruit salad. ⟶ f Chop an apple. Put it in.

3 Listen to a friend and act it out.

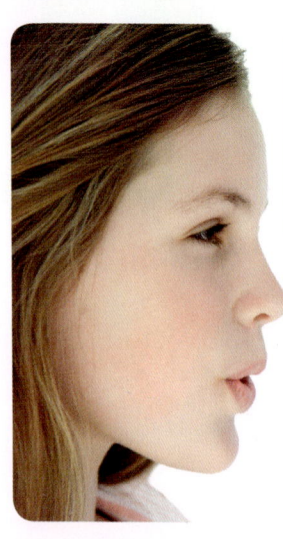

> Get a bowl for a cake.
> Get an egg. Put it in.
> Get some butter. Put it in.
> Get some meat. Throw it in!

56 Creativity

Group Check Units 3 and 4

1 How many words can you remember? Draw pictures.

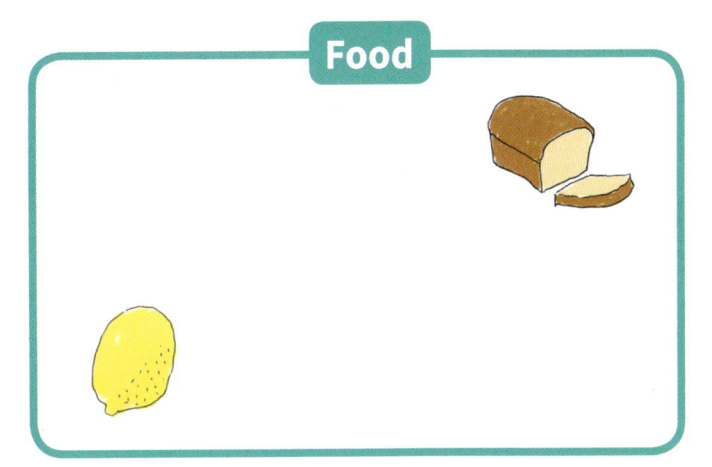

Places in a town

Food

2 Write and say the words.

3 Listen and number.

No, thank you. Can I have an apple? ☐

Sorry, there aren't any apples. But I can get apples from the shop. ☐

Yes, there is. Let's go together. ☐

OK! Thank you. Is there a shop on your street? ☐

Would you like a banana? [1]

4 Write a new dialogue. Act it out.

💬 Would you like _____?

💬 No, thank you. Can I have _____?

💬 Sorry, there aren't _____. But I can get _____ from the _____.

💬 OK! Thank you. Is there _____ your _____?

💬 Yes, there is. Let's go together.

5 My bedroom

1 🎧 061 **Listen and look. Then listen and say the words.**

1. poster
2. wardrobe
3. mirror
4. armchair
5. lamp
6. bed
7. table
8. sofa
9. rug

BIG QUESTION What does furniture look like?

2 🎧 062 **Listen and chant.**

There's a train on the sofa.
Please tidy up! OK?
There's a cap on the mirror.
Please put your things away!

There are pencils on the rug.
Please tidy up! OK?
There's a book on the wardrobe.
Please put your things away!

There are jeans on the armchair.
Please tidy up! OK?
There's a ball on the table.
Please put your things away!

There's a schoolbag on the floor.
Please tidy up! OK?
There's a sock on the poster.
Please put your things away!

58 Furniture

1 Read and match.

a I like this red lamp. ☐

b I like that blue lamp over there. ☐

c I like these green lamps. ☐

d I like those purple lamps over there. ☐

2 🔴 🎧 063 Watch, listen and say.

Language focus

I like your bedroom
And all the things in here.
I like **this** wardrobe.
I like **that** chair.

I like **these** posters
And **those** lovely lamps.
I like it so much …
I think I want to camp.

3 Play the guessing game.

I'm thinking of something blue.

Is it this pen?

Yes, it is. Your turn.

I'm thinking of something red.

Is it that chair?

This, that, these, those 59

1 🎧 064 ▶ Listen and sing. Then tick ✓ the furniture in the song.

Give me a piece of wood,
Let's see what I can do.
Let's cut and paint and make
Some furniture for you.

Take that piece of wood,
Cut it and paint it red.
Put it all together now.
Wow! I like this bed.

Give me a piece of wood,
Let's see what I can do …

Take that piece of wood,
Cut it and paint some squares.
Put it all together now.
Wow! I like these chairs.

Give me a piece of wood,
Let's see what I can do …

2 What can people make with wood? How many ideas have you got?

> People can make a … with wood.

Singing for pleasure

1 🎧 066 Listen and answer. Write *Lisa's*, *Nick's*, *Mike's* or *Emily's*.

1 Whose jumper is this?   It's _____.

2 Whose jeans are these?   They're _____.

3 Whose jumper is this?   It's _____.

4 Whose jeans are these?   They're _____.

2 ▶ 🎧 067 Watch, listen and say.

> **Language focus**
>
> **Whose** shoes **are these**?   **Whose** hat **is this**?
> **They're** Penny**'s** shoes.   **It's** Penny**'s** hat.

3 Look at the pictures. Then ask and answer.

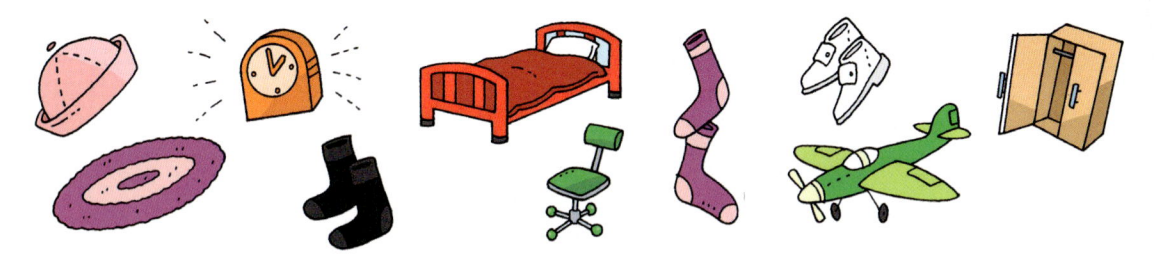

Whose hat is this?

It's May's hat.

Whose … this / these … ?

Tidy up!

1 🎧 068 ▶ **Where are the toys at the end of the story?**

1

Whisper: Hello, it's Whisper. Can Flash come to the park?
Flash's mum: Sorry Whisper, not now. She's tidying up her room.

2

Flash: I don't like tidying up. Ah, I've got an idea!

3

Flash: First the clothes – jeans, sweaters, caps, shoes and socks!

4

Flash: Now the school things and the toys! Bag, books, balls and dolls. Ha!

5

Flash: Finished! Can I go to the park now?
Flash's mum: Just a minute. Let me check first.

6

Flash's mum: Wow! The room is really tidy now.

Value: tidiness

7

Flash's mum: Oh, your T-shirt. Let's put it in the wardrobe.
Flash: No, Mum, no!

8

Flash's mum: I don't believe it!
Flash: Sorry, Mum. No park for me today.

2 Read, think and circle.

1 In picture two, Flash feels …
2 In picture five, Flash feels …
3 In picture eight, Flash feels …

Phonics

3 Find who says …

Bag, b**oo**ks, balls and dolls.

4 🎧 069 Listen and say.

L**oo**k at the b**oo**ks all over the r**oo**m.

Phonics focus: the letter sound *oo*

Skills

1 Read and write the correct words next to numbers 1–8.

desk   books   chairs   bed   posters   clock   bookcase   wardrobe

My room

In my room, there's a big yellow **(1)** _____. There's a white
(2) _____ and there's a **(3)** _____ under the window.
On it, there's my toy car. There are three **(4)** _____ on the wall.
There are also three **(5)** _____ in my room, but there isn't a
(6) _____. There's a blue **(7)** _____ next to the wardrobe.
I think there are twelve **(8)** _____ on it.

1 🎧 070 Listen and answer.

Claire goes to her …

1 Where does Claire go when she wants to think?
2 Where does she sit?
3 What does she do?
4 Where do you go when you want to think?
5 What do you do?

2 Tell a friend what you like to do in your room.

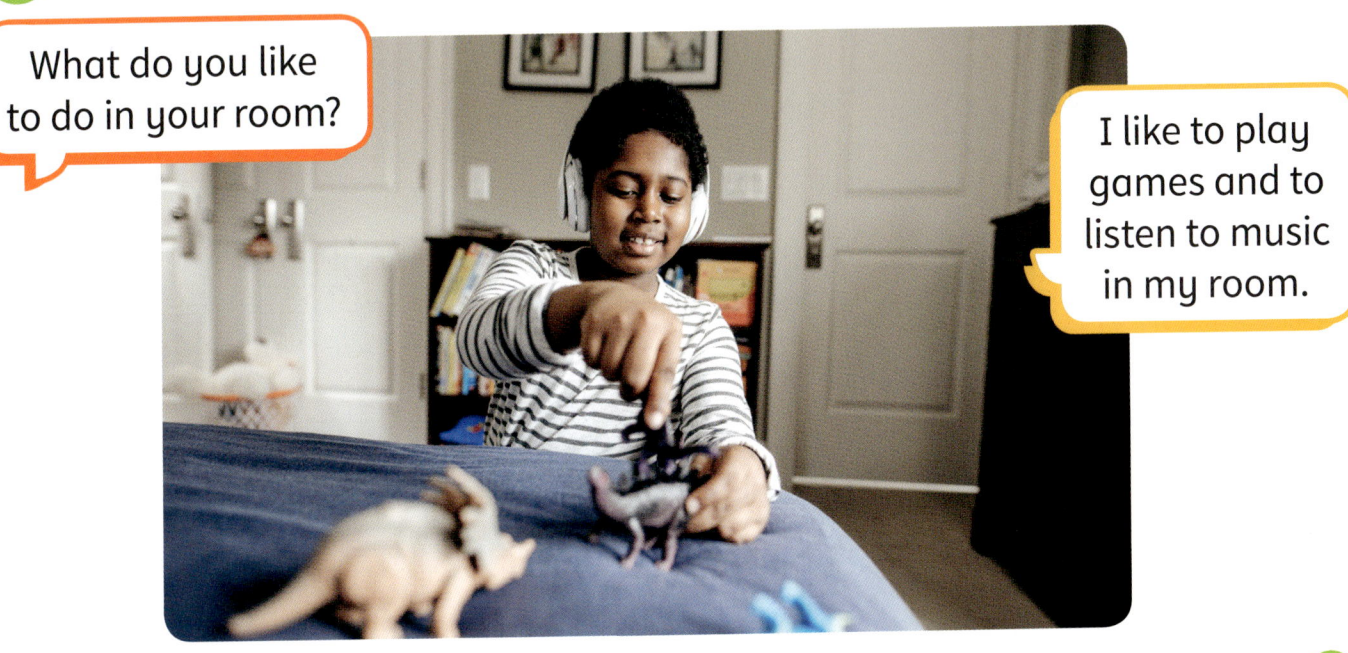

What do you like to do in your room?

I like to play games and to listen to music in my room.

Listening, speaking and writing

Think and learn

Materials

▶ **What are things made of?**

1 🎧 071 **Listen and point.**

1. wood
2. metal 
3. plastic 
4. glass 
5. fabric 

2 Look, read and tick ✓ the boxes.

There are lots of different materials. There is wood, metal, plastic, glass and fabric. We use wood to make furniture like beds and chairs. What are the things in the pictures made of?

	glass	wood	plastic	metal	fabric
1 computer			✓	✓	
2 table					
3 clock					
4 armchair					
5 lamp					
6 mirror					

3 What can this furniture be made of?

bookcase   chair
wardrobe   rug

A bookcase can be made of wood and …

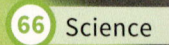

66 Science

4 In pairs, look around your classroom. Find something made of:

plastic   fabric   metal   wood   glass

This pen is made of plastic and metal. That chair is made of …

5 ⭐ Project   Draw a room you like. Label the materials.

wood • glass • wood • wood • metal • plastic • fabric • fabric • fabric • plastic

Science 67

Create that!

1 🎧 072　　Listen and imagine. Then draw your picture.

2　Work with a friend. Compare your pictures.

> In my picture, I'm sitting on …
> In your picture, you're sitting on …

68　Creativity

Think back 5

1 Read and circle.

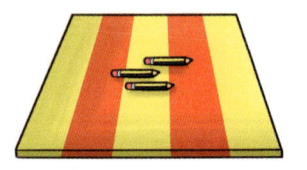

1 There are pencils on the …
  a sofa.   b rug.   c table.

2 There's a book on the …
  a wardrobe.   b lamp.   c armchair.

3 I like … lamp.
  a this   b these   c that

4 I don't like … rugs.
  a that   b these   c this

5 Whose shoes … these?
  a am   b is   c are

6 Whose jumper … this?
  a am   b is   c are

7 In the story, … can't go to the park.
  a Flash   b Whisper   c Misty

8 What are the table and chair made of?
  a wood   b glass and metal   c metal and plastic

Revision 69

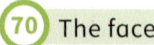

6 People

1 🎧 073 **Listen and look. Then listen and say the words.**

1. eyes
2. face
3. glasses
4. hair
5. cheeks
6. ears
7. nose
8. tears
9. chin
10. mouth

BIG QUESTION How are faces different?

2 🎧 074 **Listen and chant.**

Hair, nose, mouth, chin.
Glasses, eyes and ears.
What a pretty, pretty face.
But look there are some tears.

Hair, nose, mouth, chin.
Glasses, eyes and ears.
What a pretty, pretty face.
But look there are some tears.

The face

1 Read and write the names.

a _____ b _____ c _____

d _____ e _____ f _____

1 Henry has got short black hair. He's tired.
2 Anna's wearing glasses and has got long blonde hair. She's happy.
3 Kate has got black hair and brown eyes. She's sad.
4 Claire has got long red hair. She's wearing glasses. She's excited.
5 Luke has got long blond hair. He's got blue eyes. He's scared.
6 Julian has got short curly hair and brown eyes. He's angry.

2 075 Watch, listen and say.

Language focus

Are you angry?
No, I'm not angry.
I'm not tired.

Are you happy?
Yes, I'm happy and excited.

3 Play the mime game.

Are you … ?

Am / Is / Are + adjective 71

1 🎧 076 ▶ **Listen and sing. Then draw lines.**

**Do you know my face
Is like an open book?
You can know my feelings
From my face! Have a look!**

Sometimes I'm tired,
So I go to sleep. ○
Sometimes I'm scared,
So I hug my toy sheep. ○
Sometimes I'm tired …

**Do you know my face
Is like an open book? …**

Sometimes I'm sad
The town looks grey. ○
Sometimes I'm happy,
It's a beautiful day! ○
Sometimes I'm sad …

**Do you know my face
Is like an open book? …**

2 **Look, think and write.**

😃	😢	😠	😴	😊
I'm happy so …	I'm sad so …	I'm angry so …	I'm tired so …	I'm excited so …
I sing a lot.	I cry.	I _____	_____	_____

72 Singing for pleasure

1 🎧 **078** Listen and chant.

The months are easy to remember:
January, February, March,
April, May and June,
July, August, September,
October, November, December.
Remember? No?
Then start again: January, February …

2 🎧 **079** Listen, read and circle.

1 Ben's birthday is in **June** / **May**.

2 Lucy's birthday is in **May** / **April**.

3 Tim and Sam's birthdays are in **May** / **July**.

3 ▶ 🎧 **080** Watch, listen and say.

Language focus

Our birthdays aren't in May.
They aren't in September.
Our birthdays are in November!

Their birthdays aren't in May.
They aren't in September.
Their birthdays are in November!

4 Find out when your friends' birthdays are. Then play the birthday game.

Our birthdays are in …

Their birthdays are in …

The months, *our*, *their*

Thunder's birthday

1 🎧 081 ▶ Do Thunder, Flash and Misty win medals?

1
Flash, Whisper and Misty: Pull, pull, pull, you can win this tug of war.

2
Thunder: Oh no!
Other children: We're the winners.

3
Thunder: Let's have a three-legged race.
Whisper: Great. I want to be with Flash, please.

4
Whisper: Help!
Flash: Oh dear.
Whisper: No medal for us.

5
Thunder: Let's play *Pin the tail on the donkey*.
Misty: Great!

6
Thunder: That's perfect, Misty.
Whisper: Misty's great!

74 Value: being a good loser

7 **Thunder, Flash and Whisper:** You aren't wearing your blindfold. That's not fair!

8 **Thunder, Flash, Misty and Whisper:** No medals for us today.
Other children: Bye!

2 Look at the picture and choose the correct sentence.

1 That's not fair!
2 We're the winners!
3 Let's have a race.
4 Let's play.

Phonics

3 Find who says …

Let's pl**ay** Pin the t**ai**l on the donkey.

4 🎧 082 Listen and say.

J**a**n**e**, it's a r**ai**ny d**ay** but don't m**a**k**e** a sad f**a**c**e**, come out and pl**ay**.

Phonics focus: the letter sounds *a_e*, *ai* and *ay*

Skills

1 Read, think and write what's missing in each birthday invitation.

1

Dear Eve, _____

Can you come to my birthday party, please? Please bring your sister with you. Mia wants to play games with her.

The party is at our house — 21 Top Road. It starts at three o'clock.

See you there!

Ava

2

Dear Anthony, _____

Please come to my birthday party on Friday. Can you bring your skateboard, please? Can you come? The party starts at four o'clock.

See you on Friday.

Ella

3

Dear Barbara, _____

Come to my birthday party, please. It's on Sunday. Please bring your brother, too. I've got three new kites. We can fly them. The birthday party is in our garden - 15, Red House Road.

See you on Sunday. Hooray!

Henry

2 Write an invitation to your birthday party.

Remember to write:
where it is.
what day it is.
what time it is.

76 Reading and writing

1 🎧 083 **Listen and number.**

a

b

c

d

e

f

2 🛡️ **Draw a clown face and play the game.**

- Has your clown got … hair?
- Yes, he has.
- Has your clown got … eyes?
- No, he hasn't.

Listening and speaking

Think and learn

Portraits

▶ How do artists make faces?

1 🎧 084 Listen and point.

1. painting
2. drawing
3. photo
4. paper collage

2 Read and match the museum labels to the portraits in Activity 1.

Artists do pencil drawings and colour paintings of faces. They take photos of faces and they make collages of faces with paper and glue, too. These are all called 'portraits.'

a. For this portrait, the artist uses a grey pencil. The person in the portrait is young. The grey pencil shows the shape of her face and eyes. ☐

b. For this portrait, the artist uses a camera. The person in the portrait has big glasses and a smile. ☐

c. In this portrait, the artist uses small bits of newspapers and black crayon. ☐

d. For this portrait, the artist uses paint. It has got lots of different colours. ☐

3 Look at the portraits again. How are the people feeling?

happy   excited   scared   angry   sad   tired

I think the person in 1 is sad.

I don't. I think the person is scared.

78 Art

4 Choose one of the portraits and write a museum label for it.

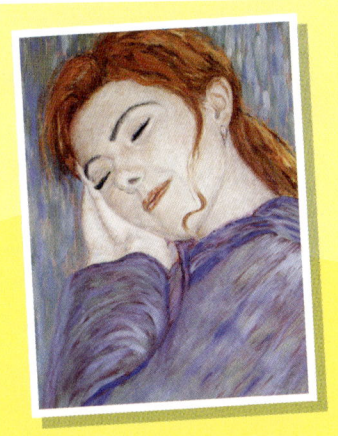

For this portrait, the artist uses ... The person is ...

5 Read your museum label to a friend. Can they guess the picture?

6 ⭐ Project Do a portrait of a person you like. Write about the portrait. Then tell a friend.

This portrait is a drawing. For my drawings, I use crayons and a pencil. The person is my brother. He's excited so his eyes are big.

Art

Do that!

1 🎧 085 **Listen and act out with your teacher. Then listen again and number the pictures.**

2 Read the sentences from the story and draw lines.

a You hear an interesting noise.

b Say 'Thank you' and smile.

c A friend gives you a birthday present.

d You're excited. Open it and see.

e It's a broken vase.

f Shake the present and listen.

3 Listen to a friend and act it out.

A friend gives you a big present. You're happy. Open it and see. It's an interesting book!

80 Creativity

Group Check Units 5 and 6

1 How many words can you remember? Draw pictures.

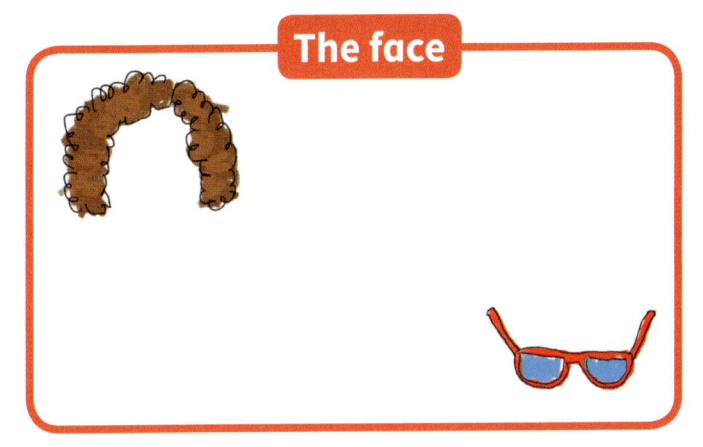

Furniture

The face

2 Write and say the words.

3 086 Listen and number.

- No, I'm very angry. Look! There are shoes on my bed. ☐
- Are you OK? **1**
- The socks are my brother's, too! ☐
- They're my brother's. ☐
- Whose are the shoes? ☐
- And whose are those socks on the lamp? ☐

4 Write a new dialogue. Act it out.

○ Are you OK?

○ _____, I'm very _____.
Look! There are _____.

○ Whose _____ ?   ○ They're _____

○ And whose _____ ?   ○ The _____

Revision 81

7 Off we go!

1. helicopter
2. ship
3. lorry
4. boat
5. scooter
6. skateboard
7. motorbike
8. taxi
9. bus

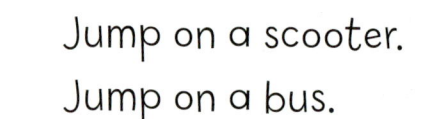

1 🎧 087 **Listen and look. Then listen and say the words.**

BIG QUESTION Where can transport go?

2 🎧 088 **Listen and chant.**

Jump on a scooter.
Jump on a bus.
Jump on a motorbike.
And come with us.

Jump on a plane.
Jump on a boat.
Jump on a skateboard.
And off we go.

Jump in a helicopter.
Jump in a car.
Jump on a bike.
Are we going far?

Jump in a taxi.
Jump on a train.
Jump in a lorry.
Let's go again!

82 Transport

1 Match the children with the pictures. Then write the words.

1 Paul — I'd like to drive a _____.

2 Mary — I'd like to fly a _____.

3 Eric — I'd like to ride a _____.

4 Ruth — I'd like to sail a _____.

a
b
c
d

2 🎧 089 Watch, listen and say.

Language focus

I**'d like to go** to Brazil by plane!

I**'d like to go** to Brazil!

I**'d like to go** to Spain by bus!

I**'d like to go** to Spain!

3 Talk about your dream holiday.

What's your dream holiday?

I'd like to go to Italy by ship. I'd like to go with my best friend.

I'd like to …

1 🎧 090 ▶ **Listen and sing. Then tick ✓ the transport in the song.**

I'd like to go to Africa.
I think it's very far.
I'd like to go there on a plane.
It's too far for a car. For a car.

Far or near, near or far.
Plane or bus, ship or car.
Transport takes us here and there.
Transport takes us everywhere.

I'd like to go to my friend's house
It's not so very far.
I'd like to go on my skateboard.
It's too close for a car. For a car.

Far or near, near or far …

I'd like to go to outer space.
I know it's very far.
I'd like to take a rocket there.
It's too far for a car. For a car.

Far or near, near or far …

2 **Ask and answer.**

school   the park   the cinema   the beach
your friend's house   Africa   the moon

What's the best way to get to school?

The best way to get to school is …

84 Singing for pleasure

7

1 Read and match.

1. What are you doing?
   I'm waiting for a taxi.

2. What's Martin doing?
   He's flying a plane.

3. What are you doing?
   I'm looking for my scooter.

4. What's Ella doing?
   She's learning to skateboard.

a
b
c
d

2 🎬 🎧 092 Watch, listen and say.

Language focus

Are you driving a bus?
No, I'm not!
Are you driving a car?
No, I'm not!

Are you driving a taxi?
Yes, I am!
What **are you doing**?
I'm driving a taxi!
Beep! Beep!

3 Play the mime game.

What are you doing?
Are you riding a bike?

Yes, I am. / No, I'm not. I'm …

Questions and answers with verb + *ing* **85**

The bus trip

1 🎧 093 ▶ Which transport can you see?

1
Flash: A day at the beach!
Thunder: I'm excited.
Misty: Off we go!

2
Misty: The bus isn't moving.
Thunder: Why?
Whisper: Let's ask the driver.

3
Driver: There are lots of sheep on the road. Look!
Whisper: No problem. I can help.

4
Whisper: We'd like to go to the beach.
Sheep: OK. Have a good day!

5
Driver: Thanks.
Whisper: No problem.

6
Driver: Oh no. We've got a problem with the tyre.
Thunder: I think I can help.

Value: being generous

7

Driver: Thanks.
Thunder: You're welcome.

8

Driver: Here we are!
Misty: Where's the beach?
Woman: What beach? This is the bus to the airport.
Driver: Now it's my turn to help you! Let's go to the beach!

2 Read and complete the text.

> Super Friends   sheep
> airport   Thunder   beach

The Super Friends would like to go to the **(1)** _____ . There's a problem with some **(2)** _____ but Whisper helps the driver. There's a problem with the tyre, but **(3)** _____ helps the driver. Then the bus arrives – but it's at the **(4)** _____ not the beach! Now the driver helps the **(5)** _____ and drives to the beach.

Phonics

3 Find who says …   *It's my turn to help y**ou**!*

4 🎧 094 Listen and say.

L**u**k**e** rides his n**ew** bl**ue** sc**oo**ter to the z**oo**.

Phonic focus: the letter sounds u_e, ew, ue and oo

Skills

1 🎧 095 　 Listen and stick.

2 Look and say.　　The bike is …

88　Listening and speaking

7

1 🎧 096 **Listen and tick ✓ the transport Monica uses.**

	Monday	Tuesday	Wednesday	Thursday	Friday
bus					
car					
bike					
taxi					

2 **Ask and answer.**

Which transport do you use?

On Tuesdays, I ride my bike to school.

3 **Read and tick ✓ the things that the car has got.**

This car is amazing because it's very long. Inside there are TVs and beds and a lot of sofas for all your friends. There is a swimming pool too! They use this car in films or for special parties.

clock ☐   TV ☐   swimming pool ☐   sofa ☐   lamp ☐   bed ☐

4 🛡 **Draw and write about an amazing car, bus, train or plane.**

This is my bus. It is blue and red. It's very big. It's got a bed in it. I'd like to go to China in it with my dad.

Listening, reading and writing

Think and learn

Transport

▶ Where does transport go?

1 🎧 097 Listen and point.

1. in the air
2. on land
3. on water

2 Where do they go? Look and tick ✓.

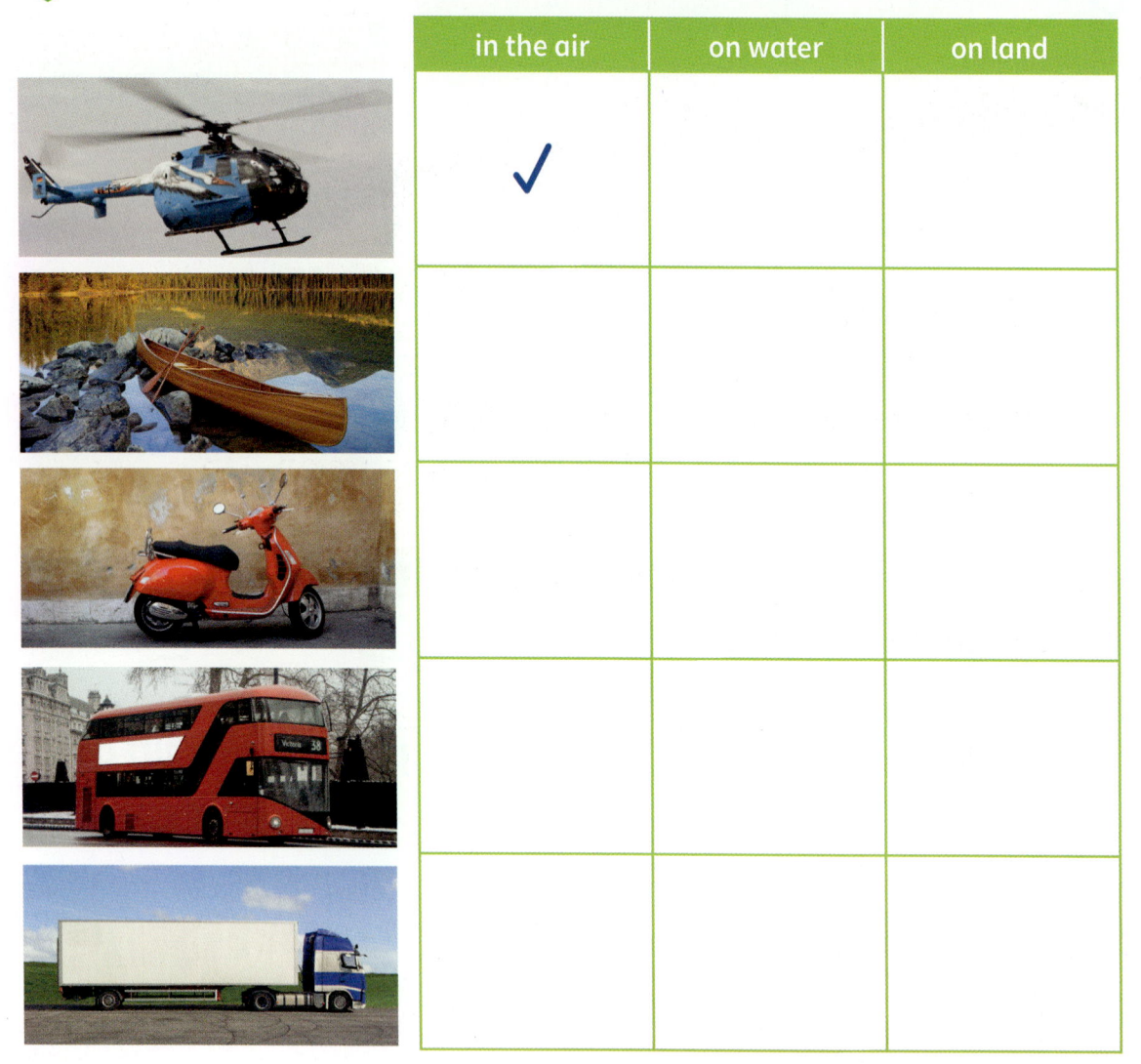

	in the air	on water	on land
helicopter	✓		
canoe			
scooter			
bus			
truck			

3 Work in pairs. Say.

A train goes …   … on land!

90 Geography

4 Work in groups. Say with your friends.

Where are they going?

In number 1, they're going to school. They can get there on ... by ... or ... .

5 ⭐ Project What transport would you like to take? Make a transport calendar.

Monday	Tuesday	Wednesday	Thursday	Friday	Saturday	Sunday

Geography

Create that!

1 🎧 098 Listen and imagine. Then draw your picture.

2 Work with a friend. Compare your pictures.

> In my picture, I'm sailing on the water …
> with my brother. I'm going by …
> In your picture, you're …

92 Creativity

Think back 7

1 Read and circle.

1. Look! I've got a new …
   a ship.   b scooter.   c rocket.

2. Look! This is my new …
   a ship.   b lorry.   c motorbike.

3. I … by plane to Brazil.
   a 'd like to go   b like to go   c like

4. I'd … to Spain with my grandpa.
   a 'd liked to go   b like to go   c like

5. I'm … a car.
   a driving   b not driving

6. I'm … to skateboard.
   a learning   b not learning

7. In the story, the friends would like to go to …
   a school.   b the airport.   c the beach.

8. Ships go …
   a on land.   b in the air.   c on water.

Revision 93

8 Sports club

1 🎧 099 **Listen and look. Then listen and say the words.**

1. badminton
2. table tennis
3. tennis
4. basketball
5. baseball
6. volleyball
7. swimming
8. football
9. hockey
10. athletics

BIG QUESTION What do we need to play sports?

2 🎧 100 **Listen and chant.**

Football, basketball,
Lots of sport to do.
Tennis, badminton.
Let's do it – me and you.

Table tennis and athletics.
That's great fun –
don't forget it.
Let's join a club today.
Let's join a club hooray.

Baseball and swimming,
Lots of sport to do.
Hockey, volleyball.
Let's do it – me and you.

Table tennis and athletics.
That's great fun –
don't forget it.
Let's join a club today.
Let's join a club hooray!

Sport

1 🎧 101 **Look and draw lines from the pictures to the sentences. Then listen and number the pictures.**

a

Swimming is fun.

c

Playing tennis is difficult.

Dancing is great.

b

Playing baseball is boring.

d

2 ▶ 🎧 102 **Watch, listen and say.**

Language focus

Playing football**'s** fun.   **Flying** a kite**'s** difficult.
Dancing's great.   But **swimming's** easy!

3 **Look and draw lines. Then ask and answer.**

flying   watching   listening to   reading

painting   making   riding   playing

What do you think about flying a kite?   Flying a kite's …

ing forms 95

1. 🎧 103 ▶ Listen and sing. Then write the words.

goal   friends   pitch   football   volleyball   court

Playing sport is easy.
It's all I want to do.
I'd like to play with you.
Playing sport is great fun.
It's all I want to do.
I'd like to play with you.

Give me a pitch,
Give me some friends,
Give me a ball to play.
Now we need two goals.
Let's play football all day.

Playing sport is easy …

Give me a court,
Give me some friends,
Give me a ball to play.
Now we need a net.
Let's play volleyball all day.

Playing sport is easy …

2. Write a new verse for the song.

Give me _____,
Give me some friends,
Give me a _____ to play.
Now we need _____
Let's play _____ all day.

96 Singing for pleasure

1 🎧 105 Listen and number the pictures.

2 ▶ 🎧 106 Watch, listen and say.

Language focus

What sport **do you like doing**?
I like playing football.
So do I.

I like playing tennis.
Me too!
like swimming.
I don't. No, no, no!

3 What are your favourite sports? Write, ask and answer.

My favourite sports:
1 _____
2 _____
3 _____

What sports do you like doing?

I like…. It's my number ….

Like + ing

The football club

1 🎧 107 ▶ What colour team are Misty and Flash in?

1
Flash: Can I join the football team?
Boy: Sorry, the team's full.

2
Misty: You can join the table tennis club.
Flash: Table tennis is boring. I like playing football.

3
Flash: I know! Let's start a football team.
Misty: OK.

4
Flash and Misty: Join our team!

5
Flash: Do you want to play a game?
Boy: Ha, ha. It's going to be very easy.

6
Thunder: Goal!
Whisper: Well done, Flash!

98 Value: including people

7

Whisper: Great goal, Misty!
Boy: Come on. Try harder, Green team.

8

Boy: Do you want to be in my team?
Flash: No, thank you. We've got our team.

2 Read and tick ✓ the boxes.

1 The boys' football team is full.   yes ☐ / no ☐
2 Flash wants to play tennis.   yes ☐ / no ☐
3 Flash and Misty start a team.   yes ☐ / no ☐
4 The boy thinks his team is going to win. yes ☐ / no ☐
5 Thunder scores a goal.   yes ☐ / no ☐

Phonics

3 Find who says … *Great g**oa**l, Misty!*

4 🎧 108 Listen and say.

A hipp**o** and a g**oa**t with a h**o**l**e** in their b**oa**t.

Phonics focus: the letter sounds *o*, *oa* and *o_e*

Skills

1 🎧 109 Listen and put a tick ✓ or a cross ✗ in the boxes.

	table tennis		badminton		hockey		skiing		athletics	
	😃	😟	😃	😟	😃	😟	😃	😟	😃	😟
Sue										
Henry										

2 Ask and answer.

> How many children like swimming?

> Eight children like swimming.

swimming IIIII III
football IIIII II

3 Now write about your class and make a bar chart.

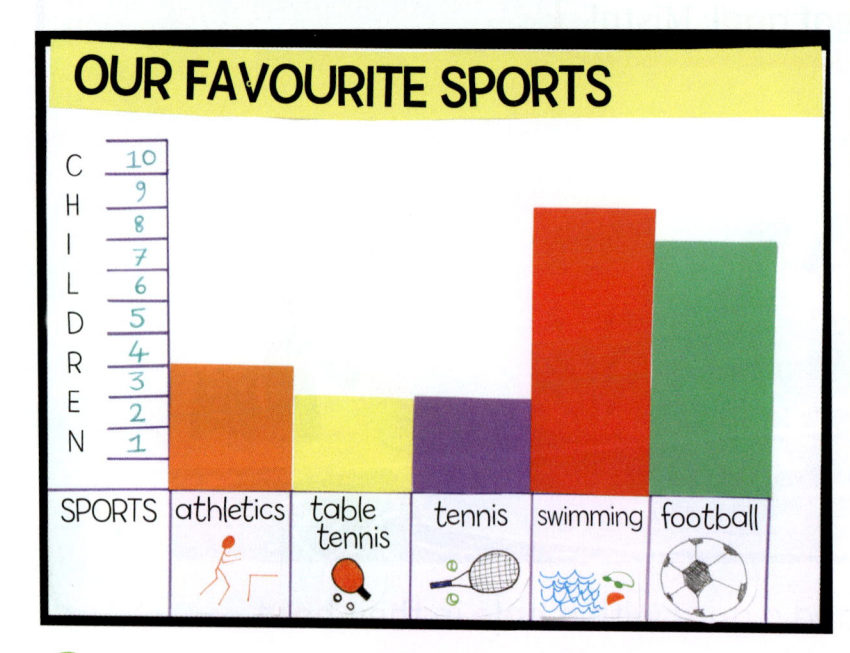

OUR FAVOURITE SPORTS

CHILDREN: 1–10

SPORTS: athletics, table tennis, tennis, swimming, football

In our class there are 22 children.
8 children's favourite sport is swimming.
7 children's favourite sport is football.
3 children's favourite sport is athletics.
2 children's favourite sport is table tennis.
2 children's favourite sport is tennis.

1 Look and read. Write *yes* or *no*.

1 The children are in a park. _____

2 There are 13 children. _____

3 The girls are playing volleyball. _____

4 The girls in one team are wearing blue T-shirts. _____

5 Four children are swimming. _____

6 Two boys are playing table tennis. _____

Think and learn

Sports equipment

▶ What do we need to play sports?

1 🎧 110 Listen and point.

1. bat
2. racket
3. helmet
4. board
5. goggles
6. net

2 Look at the table and tick ✓. Say sentences about the sports.

	ball	bat	racket	board	helmet	net	goggles
baseball	✓	✓			✓		
basketball							
tennis							
snowboarding							
swimming							

> For baseball, we need a helmet, a ball and a bat.

3 What equipment do we need for these sports?

table tennis   football   surfing   volleyball

102 Physical education

4 🎧 111 Write the sport next to where we play it.
Then listen and check.

football   badminton   basketball
ride a bike   hockey   tennis
athletics   running   baseball

court

track

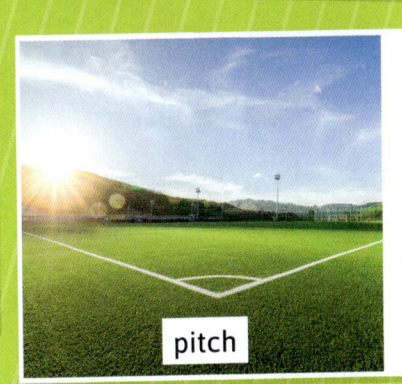

pitch

5 ⭐ Project Make a leaflet about your favourite sport.

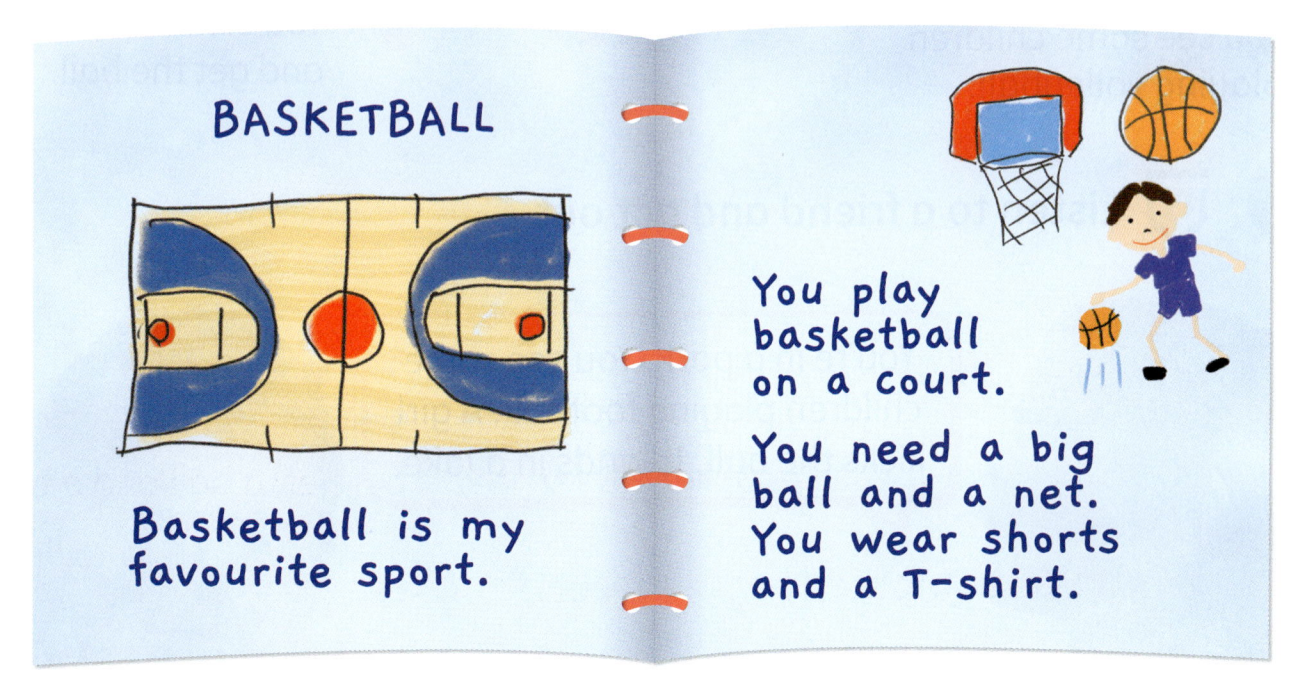

BASKETBALL

Basketball is my favourite sport.

You play basketball on a court.

You need a big ball and a net. You wear shorts and a T-shirt.

Physical education 103

Do that!

1 🎧 112 **Listen and act out with your teacher. Then listen again and number the pictures.**

2 Read the sentences from the story and draw lines.

a You say, 'Can I play with you, please?'

b You hit the ball. It lands in a tree.

c The children are happy. They give you a high five.

d You're on a beach.

e You see some children playing volleyball.

f You climb up the tree and get the ball.

3 🛡 **Listen to a friend and act out.**

> You're in a park. You see some children playing football. A girl kicks the ball. It lands in a lake.

104 Creativity

Group Check Units 7 and 8

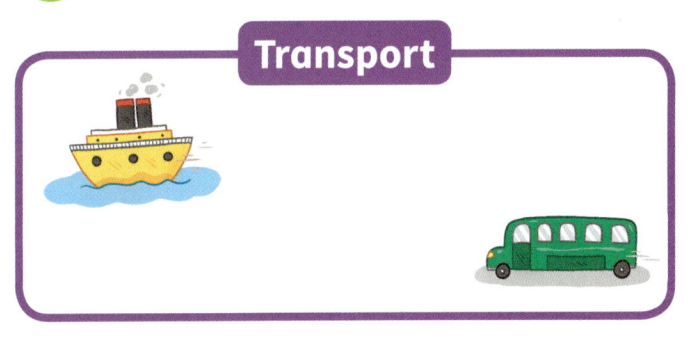

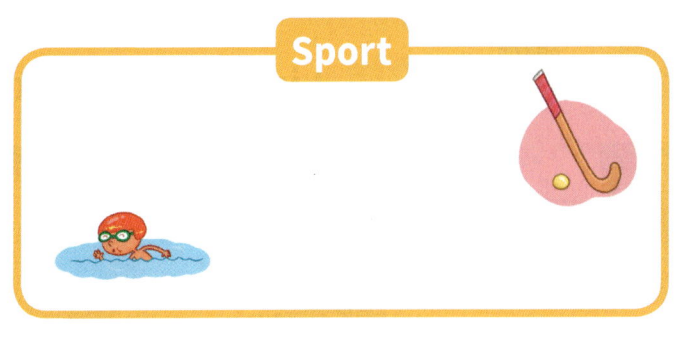

1 How many words can you remember? Draw pictures.

Transport

Sport

2 Write and say the words.

3 🎧 113 Listen and number.

So do I. I'd like to go swimming on Saturday. ☐

I don't. Playing badminton's difficult. ☐

I like playing badminton. ☐

Me too! Let's go together. ☐

I also like swimming. ☐

What sports do you like doing? [1]

4 Write a new dialogue. Act it out.

💬 What sports do you like doing?

💬 I also _____.

💬 I like _____.

💬 So do I. _____.

💬 I don't. _____.

💬 Me too! _____.

Revision

9 Holiday plans

1 🎧 114 Listen and look. Then listen and say the words.

1. read a comic
2. go hiking
3. visit cousins
4. help in the garden
5. take riding lessons
6. build a tree house
7. keep a scrapbook
8. learn to swim
9. go camping

BIG QUESTION What makes a good holiday?

2 🎧 115 Listen and chant.

Give me a **G**!
Go camping.
Give me an **H**!
Help in the garden.
Give me a **V**!
Visit my cousins.
Give me a **K**!
Keep a scrapbook.

Give me an **L**!
Learn how to swim.
Give me a **B**!
Build a tree house.
Give me a **G**!
Go hiking.
Give me an **H**!
Holiday! **H**oliday! **H**oliday!

1 🎧 116 Look, read and write the names. Then listen and check.

Maisy   Ryan   Elsie   Toby

1 Can I take a riding lesson on Monday? _____
2 Can I help you in the garden on Wednesday? _____
3 Can we go camping on Friday? _____
4 Can we go hiking on Sunday? _____

2 ▶ 🎧 117 Watch, listen and say.

Language focus

Can I build a tree house?
Yes, of course you can.
Can I take riding lessons?
Yes, of course you can.

Can we go fishing?
Yes, of course we can.

3 Do a role play.

Can I build a tree house at the weekend?

Yes, you can. / No, you can't.

Can for requests 107

1 🎧 118 ▶ **Listen and sing. Then write the numbers.**

We all need a holiday.
A time for play and rest.
Sun and sea – come with me,
Holidays are the best.
Holidays are the best.

Can we build a tree house? ☐
Can we skip and run? ☐
Can we visit cousins? ☐
We want to have some fun.
We want to have some fun.

We all need a holiday ...

Can we read a comic? ☐
Can we bake a cake? ☐
Can we keep a scrapbook? ☐
We want to have a break.
We want to have a break.

We all need a holiday ...

2 **Ask and answer.**

What makes a good holiday?

Having lots of fun.

Going to new places.

108 Singing for pleasure

1 🎧 120 Read and match. Then listen and check.

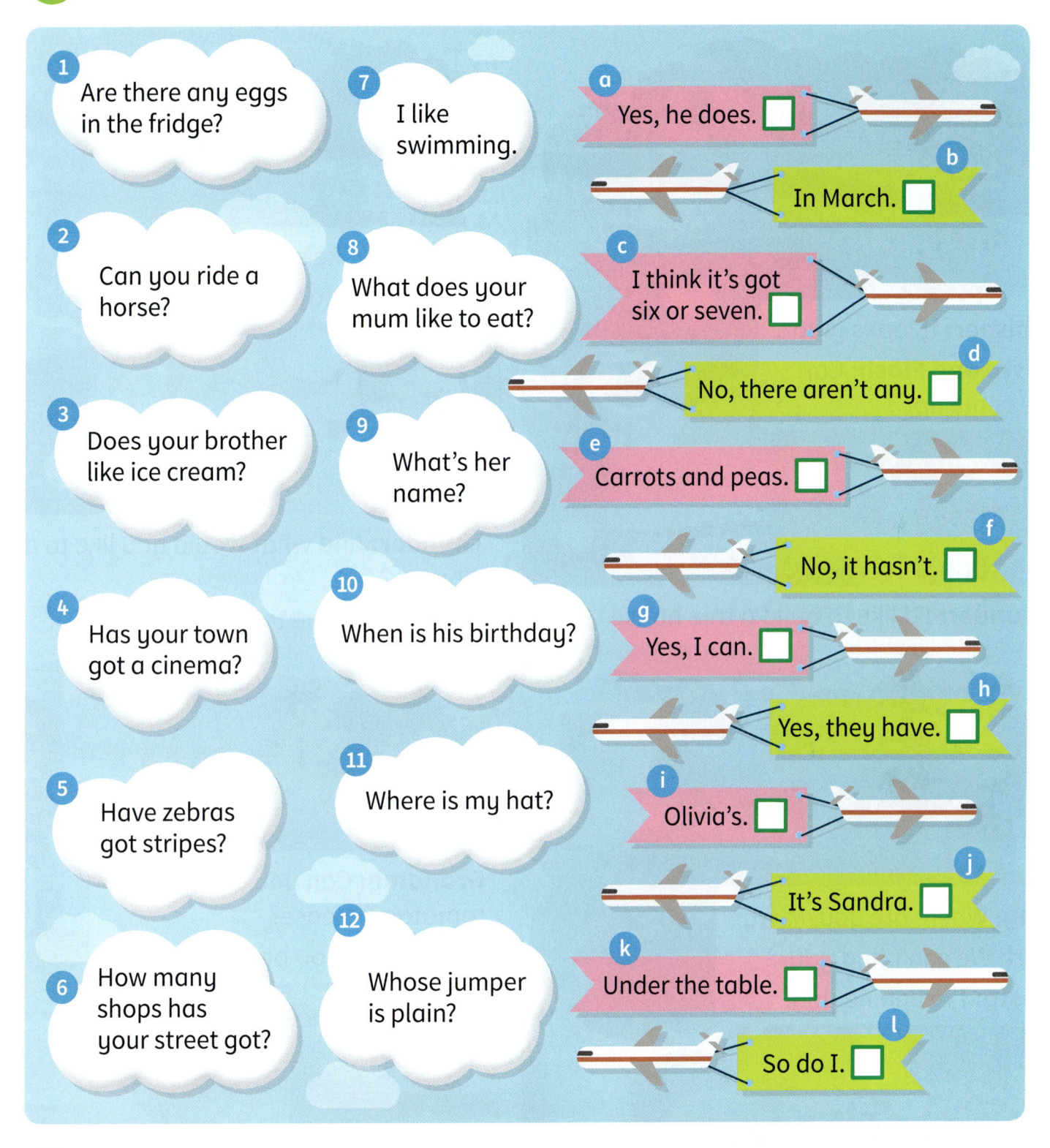

1. Are there any eggs in the fridge?
2. Can you ride a horse?
3. Does your brother like ice cream?
4. Has your town got a cinema?
5. Have zebras got stripes?
6. How many shops has your street got?
7. I like swimming.
8. What does your mum like to eat?
9. What's her name?
10. When is his birthday?
11. Where is my hat?
12. Whose jumper is plain?

a. Yes, he does.
b. In March.
c. I think it's got six or seven.
d. No, there aren't any.
e. Carrots and peas.
f. No, it hasn't.
g. Yes, I can.
h. Yes, they have.
i. Olivia's.
j. It's Sandra.
k. Under the table.
l. So do I.

2 Play the question game.

I like swimming.

So do I.

Revision

Dream holidays

1 🎧 121 ▶ What would Flash like to do?

1

Whisper: It looks great.
Misty and Flash: Can we come up?
Thunder: I'd like to build a tree house.

2

Whisper: I like swimming.
Dolphin: Me too!
Thunder: And what would you like to do, Whisper?
Whisper: I'd like to learn to swim.

3

Boy: Where are you, Misty?
Girl: We can't find you.
Misty: I'm behind you!
Whisper: What would you like to do, Misty?
Misty: I'd like to visit my cousins.

4

Grandma: Can you get me the tomatoes, please?
Flash: Here you are, Grandma.
Misty: What about you, Flash?
Flash: I'd like to help my grandma in the garden.

110 Value: teamwork

5

Teacher: Come with me, kids.

6

Teacher: Happy holiday!
Misty: Thank you very much.
Everyone: Hurray!

2 Read and write who says …

1 I'd like to help my grandma. _____

2 I'd like to learn to swim. _____

3 I'd like to build a tree house. _____

4 I'm behind you! _____

Phonics

3 Find who says …

I'd like to vi**s**it my cou**s**in**s**.

4 🎧 122 Listen and say.

My cou**s**in**s** and I are giving li**z**ard**s** banana**s** at the **z**oo.

Phonic focus: the letter sounds *z* and *s* — 111

Skills

1 Look and read. Put a tick ✓ or cross ✗ in the box.

1. This is a tiger. ☐

2. This is a watermelon. ☐

3. This is a lamp. ☐

4. This is a bus stop. ☐

5. This is a helicopter. ☐

6. This is hockey. ☐

1 🎧 123 Listen and stick.

2 Look at Activity 1. Answer the questions.

1 How many children are there in the picture?

2 What's the girl in the green dress doing?

3 What colour is the horse?

4 There's a boy eating an ice-cream. What colour are his shorts?

5 What are the children in yellow T-shirts doing?

> There are … children in the picture.

Listening and speaking

Think and learn

Helping the environment

▶ How can we help the environment on holiday?

1 🎧 124 **Listen and point.**

1. natural environment
2. recycle (recycling bin)
3. rubbish
4. path

2 Read and tick ✓ the best environment holiday picture.

Help the environment and have a good holiday:
- Recycle your rubbish in a bin or take it home. Don't leave your rubbish on the ground!
- Learn about the animals and their environment, but don't touch or play with them.
- Walk on the path. Don't walk on the plants and flowers.

1.
2.

3 What can you recycle on holiday?

You can recycle plastic bottles.

114 Environmental studies

4 Look and draw. What's good 😊 or bad 😔 for the environment on holiday?

1 We recycle our rubbish. ◯
2 We go hiking and walk on the plants. ◯
3 We go camping and we walk on the paths. ◯
4 We keep a holiday scrapbook about the environment. ◯
5 It's fun to play with animals in their habitats. ◯
6 We don't recycle bottles on holiday. ◯

5 ⭐ Project Choose a place to go on holiday. Make a scrapbook page. Use the questions to help you.

- What habitat is it?
- What animals live there?
- How can you help the environment on your holiday?
- Find some photos for your project.

My holiday

Habitat: beach and sea
Animals: birds, fish
Do:
- recycle rubbish
- take photos
- learn about the environment

Don't:
- throw rubbish on the beach or in the sea
- give food to the fish and birds
- touch the birds and fish

Environmental studies

Create that!

1 🎧 125 🛡 **Listen and imagine. Then draw your picture.**

2 **Work with a friend. Compare your pictures.**

> In my picture, I'd like to … with … .
> In your picture, you'd like to …

Creativity

Think back 9

1 Read and circle.

1. Let's ... camping.
   a keep   b go   c visit

2. Let's ... a tree house.
   a build   b help   c take

3. Let's ... to swim.
   a read   b go   c learn

4. Dad, ... I take a riding lesson on Wednesday?
   a do   b can

5. ... read a comic today?
   a I can   b Can I

6. Mum, can we ... Grandpa on Sunday?
   a visiting   b visit

7. In the story, ... would like to visit her cousins.
   a Flash   b Flash's grandma   c Misty

8. I help the environment on holiday by ...
   a respecting nature.   b walking on plants.
   c playing with animals.

Revision 117

Back to school

There's / There are ...

There's a cap on the floor.
There are some pictures on the wall.
There's a bed by the door.
But that's not all, that's not all.

There's a bookcase with some books.
Come closer. Take a look.
There's a big clock. **There's a** chair.
Can you guess who's there?

1 Read and write *There's* or *There are*.

1 _____ a bag.
2 _____ some pencils.
3 _____ some pens.
4 _____ a pencil case.
5 _____ some rubbers.

Imperatives

Open the book. **Open** the book, please.
Stand up. Stand up, please.
Don't sit down! **Don't** sit down, please!
Yes! Good dog, good dog!

2 Look and write the words.

1 **e n O p** _____ your book!
2 **a n t S d** _____ up, please!
3 **t o n' D** _____ sit down!

1 My day

Telling the time

When do you have breakfast?
At eight **o'clock**.

What's the time?
It's eight **o'clock**.

1 Look and match.

1 It's six o'clock.
2 It's seven o'clock.
3 It's eight o'clock.
4 It's nine o'clock.

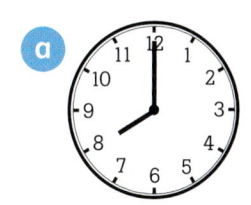

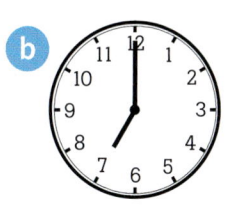

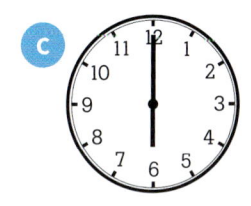

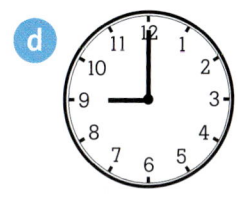

Present simple, 3rd person

Penny **walks home** at seven o'clock.
She **has her dinner** at eight.
Then she **watches some TV**
And **goes to bed**. It's late!

She's very tired at nine o'clock.
She **goes to sleep** at ten.
She **sleeps and sleeps** and then
It's time to get up again!

2 Complete the sentences.

1 Amelie _____ (get up) at six o'clock.
2 She _____ (have) breakfast at eight o'clock.
3 She _____ (go) to school at nine o'clock.
4 She _____ (play) in the park at five o'clock.

Unit 1: Language focus 119

2 The zoo

likes / doesn't like

Penny **likes** fish.
She **doesn't like** peas.

Penny **likes** fish.
She **doesn't like** cheese.

1 Read and circle.

1 Zoe the zebra **likes** / **doesn't like** sausages. 😔
2 Zak the zebra **likes** / **doesn't like** apples. 😃
3 Paula the polar bear **likes** / **doesn't like** fish. 😃
4 Peter the polar bear **likes** / **doesn't like** pizza. 😔

Questions and answers with Does … like?

Does Penny **like** crocodiles?
No, she **doesn't**.

Does Penny **like** polar bears?
Yes, she **does**!

2 Read, look and write.

                      Yes No

1 Does Zoe like parrots? ✓ ☐ _____, she _____.
2 Does Zak like tigers? ☐ ✓ _____, he _____.
3 Does Paula like monkeys? ✓ ☐ _____, she _____.
4 Does Peter like hippos? ☐ ✓ _____, he _____.

3 Where we live

Has ... got ... ?

Has your town **got** a cinema?
No, it **hasn't**!

Has your town **got** a swimming pool?
Yes, it **has**!

1 Answer the questions. What has Littletown got?

✓ 1 Has Littletown got a park? _____, it _____.
✗ 2 Has Littletown got a cinema? _____, it _____.
✓ 3 Has Littletown got a playground? _____, it _____.
✗ 4 Has Littletown got a train station? _____, it _____.

Prepositions

The fish is **next to** the rock.
The fish is **in front of** the rock.
The fish is **behind** the rock.
The fish is **between** the tree and the rock.

2 Look and write.   behind   between   in front of   next to

1 The tree is _____ the cinema.
2 The car is _____ the café.
3 The café is _____ the school and the cinema.
4 The train station is _____ the hospital.

Unit 3: Language focus 121

4 The market

Would you like … ?

Would you **like** a pizza, Penny?
Yes, please.

Would you **like** some ice cream?
No, thank you. I think I need my bed.

1 Write the questions.

1 you / Would / like / an / apple / ? _____
2 like / beans / you / Would / some / ? _____
3 egg / like / Would / an / you / ? _____
4 some / you / chicken / like / Would / ? _____

Are there / Is there any … ?

Is there any cheese in the house?
No, there **isn't any**.
Yes, there **is**.

Are there any grapes in the house?
No, there **aren't any**.
Yes, there **are**.

2 Complete the sentences and circle.

1 _____ there any kiwis in the house?   Yes, there **is** / **are**.
2 _____ there any bread in the house?   No, there **isn't** / **aren't**.
3 _____ there any milk in the house?   Yes, there **is** / **are**.
4 _____ there any potatoes in the house? No, there **isn't** / **aren't**.
5 _____ there any mangoes in the house? Yes, there **is** / **are**.

Unit 4: Language focus

5 My bedroom

this, that, these, those

I like **this** wardrobe.
I like **that** chair.

I like **these** posters.
And **those** lovely lamps.

1 Read and complete with *this*, *that*, *these* or *those*.

1 I like _____ rug here.

2 I like _____ sofa over there.

3 I like _____ lamps here.

4 I like _____ posters over there.

Whose … is this? / Whose … are these?

Whose shoes **are these**?
They're Penny**'s** shoes.

Whose hat **is this**?
It's Penny**'s** hat.

2 Read and circle.

1 Whose football **is this** / **are these**?   It's / They're Ben's football.

2 Whose socks **is this** / **are these**?   It's / They're Alice's socks.

3 Whose baseball cap **is this** / **are these**?   It's / They're Sam's baseball cap.

4 Whose trainers **is this** / **are these**?   It's / They're Eva's trainers.

5 Whose jeans **is this** / **are these**?   It's / They're Dan's jeans.

6 Whose jacket **is this** / **are these**?   It's / They're Grace's jacket.

6 People

Am / Is / Are + adjective

Are you **angry**?

No, I**'m not angry**. I**'m not tired**.

Are you **happy**?

Yes, I**'m happy** and **excited**.

1 Look and match.

1 Are you excited?
2 Is Mark angry?
3 Are you angry?
4 Is Sue happy?

a Yes, she's very happy.
b No, he isn't angry. He's tired.
c Yes, I'm excited and happy.
d No, I'm not angry. I'm sad.

The months, *our*, *their*

Our birthdays aren't in May.
They aren't in September.
Our birthdays are in November!

Their birthdays aren't in May.
They aren't in September.
Their birthdays are in November!

2 Look and complete.

December   Their   Our   June

1 _____ birthdays aren't in December. They're in _____.

2 _____ birthdays aren't in June. They're in _____.

124 Unit 6: Language focus

7 Off we go!

I'd like to ...

> **I'd like to go** to Brazil by plane!
> **I'd like to go** to Brazil!
> **I'd like to go** to Spain by bus!
> **I'd like to go** to Spain!

1 Read and complete.

> ride   drive   sail   fly

1 I'd like to _____ a helicopter.
2 I'd like to _____ a motorbike.
3 I'd like to _____ a ship.
4 I'd like to _____ a taxi.

Questions and answers with verb + *ing*

> **Are you driving** a bus?
> No, I'm not!
> **Are you driving** a car?
> No, I'm not!
>
> **Are you driving** a taxi?
> Yes, I am!
> What **are you doing**?
> **I'm driving** a taxi! Beep! Beep!

2 Read and write.

1 Are you driving a lorry?   Yes, I _____.
2 Are you sailing a boat?   No, I _____.
3 Are you flying a plane?   Yes, I _____.
4 Are you riding a scooter?   No, I _____.
5 What are you doing?   I _____ (ride) a bike.

Unit 7: Language focus

8 Sports club

ing forms

> **Playing** football**'s** fun.
> **Dancing's** great.
>
> **Flying** a kite**'s** difficult.
> But **swimming's** easy!

1 Look and write sentences.

1 great. / 's / Singing _____
2 is / athletics / fun. / Doing _____
3 baseball / Playing / difficult. / is _____
4 easy. / Dancing / 's _____

like + ing

> What sport **do you like doing**?
> I **like playing** football.
> **So do I**.
>
> I **like playing** tennis.
> **Me too**!
> I **like swimming**.
> **I don't**. No, no, no!

2 Complete the sentences.   going   playing   swimming   doing   playing

Tim What sports do you like **(1)** _____ at the weekend?

Kim I like **(2)** _____ to the park with my friends and
(3) _____ football. What about you?

Tim I like **(4)** _____ tennis. And in summer, I like
(5) _____ in the sea!

Kim So do I.

Unit 8: Language focus

9 Holiday plans

Can for requests

Can I build a tree house?
Yes, of course you can.

Can we go fishing?
Yes, of course we can.

1 Read, complete and write.

Can   build   take   keep   Can

	Yes	No	
1 Can I _____ a scrapbook?	✓	☐	_____, of course you _____.
2 _____ we go camping this weekend?	☐	✓	_____, we _____.
3 Can I _____ riding lessons?	☐	✓	_____, you _____.
4 Can we _____ a tree house?	✓	☐	_____, of course we _____.
5 _____ I go fishing?	☐	✓	_____, you _____.

Revision

2 Match the questions and answers.

1 Has your town got a swimming pool? ☐
2 Would you like some pizza? ☐
3 What's the time? ☐
4 Are there any apples in the house? ☐
5 Can I read a comic? ☐
6 Whose shoes are those? ☐
7 Does Emma like hippos? ☐
8 What sport do you like doing? ☐
9 Is there any milk in the fridge? ☐
10 What time do you have breakfast? ☐

a Yes, she does.
b Yes, of course you can.
c Yes, please.
d No, there isn't.
e No, it hasn't.
f It's three o'clock.
g They're Lucy's.
h At seven o'clock.
i Yes, there are.
j I like playing table tennis.

Unit 9: Language focus

UNIT 2 page 29

UNIT 3 page 37

UNIT 4 page 49

UNIT 7 page 88

UNIT 9 page 113